YOU CAN BRI.

RABBI SHIMON KESSIN

© Copywrite 2005, Rabbi Shimon Kessin

**Published BeSiyata Dishmaya by
PowerJews.com**

In Memory of

Zev Dovid ben HaRav Shimon HaLevi

ON THE AUTHORSHIP OF THIS WORK

On August 13, 2005, the Israeli army closed Gush Katif to the Israeli public. Two days later, forced evacuations of the Israeli residents of Gush Katif began. The legislation leading up to this and the expulsion of our brethren from their land and homes left a huge part of Israel's population in a palpable state of depression, questioning how the government could treat their own in such a heartless manner. An overwhelming urge overcame Rov Kessin to address the depression and express what can be done in response to this terrible situation. Within two weeks, the attached booklet was authored, *lishma* – anonymously! With approbations from *Gedolay Yisroel* in hand, (included herein), funding was raised to have, literally, hundreds of thousands of booklets printed and distributed throughout our Jewish Homeland. The response to this work was overwhelmingly positive, and it was successful in helping to establish a proper value system regarding to the issues of Ahavas Yisroel (loving our fellow Jew) and *Shmiras HaLashon* (proper speech) among many Israelis.

With the expansion of the internet and its ability to move information around the world effortlessly, this is the second time since 2005 that this work is being circulated to hopefully countless among our Jewish 'family' worldwide. It is the first time Rov Kessin, SHLIT'A, has consented to be identified as its author. May this work be a source of spiritual strength to all who learn it, and may it be the "*Zechus* – merit" needed to transform the *Geulah* from a dream into a vibrant reality.

It should be noted that this work was authored anonymously, which is why the approbations do not credit any person in particular but focus exclusively on the quality and intent of the book.

TRANSLATED APPROBATION FROM HaRAV MOISHE STERNBUCH, SHLIT'A

"I have received and read this (booklet), and I see that great effort is being made to rescue everyone from the sin of slander and talebearing. In short, precise, and understandable language, the author brings the (heavy) weight of this sin, its consequences, and the positive merits of guarding against this. Furthermore, the prayer to be recited daily will deliver us from this sin, and Hashem will thereby help us with all our needs.

It is worthwhile knowing that because of the grave consequences and damage this (sin) does to the Congregation and the individual, the evil inclination works hard to remove everyone's mind from how bad this sin is. I heard from a particular Godol that we accepted upon ourselves to be as careful regarding what comes out of our mouths as we are about what we put in our mouths, (kosher food), we would all be worthy of great wealth, success, and our great Geulah.

With great strength, the (anonymous) author has distributed this work free of charge, and everyone should bring this into their home. Everyone should read (and learn) it. And, with Hashem's help, we should be worthy of a great and positive Divine Influence. Hashem, the Master of Mercy, should guard us from everything negative, and those who guard what they say should be worthy of great goodness and guarded from all distress.

I anxiously wait for Hashem's Deliverance and Heaven's grand mercy."

RABBI MOISHE STERNBUCH
CHIEF RABBI
and Vice President of
the Orthodox Rabbinical Courts
JERUSALEM

Rechov Moshkovits 13 Har-Nof Jerusalem 02-651-9610

משה שטרנבוך
ראב"ד
לכל מקהילות יאשכנזים
וקרש הסוח ודרש לסכב יהושעת
שפר תג'ל, ירד"ר גבול הסדר ח"ז כ"ז
מב' כ' נשיא הועד העולמי
סקהיר ירושלים תו'

בעזהי"ת, ביום א' לפרשת "בקנאו את קנאתי בתוכם" ה'תשס"ה פעיה"ק

קבלתי הספר וקראתיו בו, וראיתי תועלת רבה בזה לכל אחד לינצל מאיסור לשון הרע ורכילות. בלשון צח וקל ובקיצור נמרץ מביא חומר האיסור וענשו ר"ל, ותועצות שיכל לזכות לכל טוב בעזיה"י, וכן מעתיק נוסח התפלה להתפלל כל יום שיינצל מהאיסור, והשי"ת יעזור לו בכל צרכיו.

וראוי לידע שדווקא מפני ענשו החמור ונזקו לציבור וליחיד, חיצר הרע משתדל שכל אחד יסיח דעתו מחומר האיסור, ויפה שמעתי מגדול אחד זצ"ל שקבלה בידו שאם ישראל היו זהירים בפה, במה שיצא במו במה שנכנס (מאכלות האסורות), היינו זוכים לאושר והצלחה וגאולה שלימה.

לכן הבה נחזיק טובה למו"ל הקונטרס הזה, ומפיצים אותו בחנם, וכל **אחד ישתדל להכניס בתוך ביתו, לקרוא בו הוא ובני ביתו, ויראה** בעזה"י תשועה מרובה ותועלת, והקב"ה בעל הרחמים ישמור אותו מכל רע, ויזכה לרב טוב וישומר פיו ולשונו שומר מצרות נפשו.

והנני מצפה בכליון ממש לישועת ה' ורחמי שמים מרובים,

[signature] [seal]

רח' משקוביץ 13, הר-נוף, ירושלים ת"ו, טל: 02-651-9610

הסכמה ניתנה לספרנו "כח הפה היהודי" שהוא הספר הנוכחי בלשה"ק.
והופץ בחינם בכל רחבי ארץ ישראל בלמעלה מ-350,000 עותקים.
וברשותו אנו מדפיסים את הסכמתו הנ"ל במהדורה זו.

TRANSLATED APPROBATION FROM
HaRAV CHAIM PINCHAS SCHEINBERG, ZT'L

"This important and honored book, filled with Hashem's Blessings, was brought to me. It is a collection of guidance and laws regarding the subject of guarding one's speech, assembled knowledgably and in good taste by a Talmudic scholar. Coming from a vaad associated with "Tzipiso l'Yeshua" (waiting for the Geulah), the author has gathered ideologies in (the realm of) Mussar and Jewish philosophies based in the G-d fearing words of our Sages as they relate to guarding one's speech, slander, talebearing, and how careful we need be regarding this. Every person is, as a member of the Congregation, is responsible to observe this. This book is filled with words of strength regarding how to safeguard our speech. There is no doubt that this book provides great help, and anyone who brings it into their home, (learning & living it), brings great blessing into their home as well."

מכתבי ברכה מאת הרבנים הגאונים שליט"א

Rabbi CHAIM P. SCHEINBERG
Rosh Hayeshiva "TORAH ORE"
and Morah Hora'ah of Kiryat Mattersdorf

הרב חיים פינחס שיינברג
ראש ישיבת "תורה אור"
ומורה הוראה דקרית מטרסדורף

בס"ד, חודש תמוז, תשס"ה

מכתב ברכה

הנה הובא לפני ספר חשוב ונכבד, מלא ברכת ה', ליקוט מוסר והלכות בעניני שמירת הלשון, אשר ערכו בטוב טעם ודעת חבר תלמידי חכמים שליט"א, במכון החשוב אשר בשם "צפית לישועה" מכונה, והוא ליקוט רעיונות במוסר, מחשבה ויראת ה' מדברי רבותינו בענין שמירת הלשון, ובדיני לשון הרע ורכילות, והזהירות הרבה בהם, עם האחריות הגדולה לכל אחד מהכלל בעניינים אלו, וספר זה מלא בדברי חיזוק לשמירת הדיבור, וללא ספק תהיה תועלת מרובה מספר זה, והמביא ספר זה לתוך ביתו מביא לביתו ברכה מרובה.

ועל כן אברך את הרבנים המתעסקים בענין חשוב זה שיזכה וספרם זה יתקבל באהבה ובשמחה לפני עם ישראל קדושים, ויתרבה כבוד ה' ותורתו בעולם.

הכו"ח לכבד התורה ולומדיה

רחוב פנים מאירות 2, ירושלים, ת.ד. 6979, טל. 537-1513 (02), ישראל
2 Panim Meirot St., Jerusalem, P.O.B. 6979, Tel. (02) 537-1513, Israel

TRANSLATED APROBATION FROM JERUSALEM'S BEIT DIN HaTZEDEK

"Our Court has been asked to address the great Mitzvah that is addressed in every language regarding the author who has devoted his heart and soul to strengthening the masses and making them worthy regarding the (observance of) loving our fellow Jew and guarding our tongue.

The important operation of our time is based in revealing the grand importance of these subjects. Great effort is invested to promote the value in strengthening ourselves regarding how we speak. We must be more vigilant regarding the stringency of how bad this sin is, especially as it relates to the sin of hating our fellow Jew. That (attitude) leads to slander and talebearing.

It is a great Mitzvah to participate in this with our entire heart and soul and to help in any way we can. It is the desire of Hashem to place in our hands the ability to succeed and strengthen our generation, to overcome these (sins) more than anything else. The merit is so great that it will protect our Holy Nation from every pain and trouble.

In the merit of this great effort, and in the merit of Chofetz Chaim, ZT'L, Hashem will guard us and all Israel, bringing the Geulah quickly in our days."

BETH DIN ZEDEK
OF THE ORTHODOX
COMMUNITY JEWISH
JERUSALEM E. ISRAEL
26 STRAUSS ST.
P.O.B 5006 FAX 6221317 TL.0246345

בית דין צדק
לכל מקהלות האשכנזים
שע"י "העדה החרדית"
פעיה"ק ירושלם תובב"א
ת.ד. 5006 פאקס 6221317 טל. 6252608

ע"ה שבט תשס"ב

הסכמה והמלצה

הביד"צ דפעיה"ק ת"ו נמנים לדבר מצוה רבה לעורר בכל לשון לסייע בידי המוסד החשוב... שבראשות הרב הגאון... שליט"א המסורים בלב ונפש לזכות את הרבים בענין אהבת ישראל ושמירת הלשון.

ועד המבצע החשוב שעוסקים כעת לפרסם גודל הענינים האלה, ומשקיעים בזהות להודיע גודל התועלת של ההתחזקות בשמירת הלשון ולקבל על עצמם תוספת זהירות בחומר האיסור של שנאת חנם והחמא החמור של לשה"ר ורכילות ר"ל.

ומצוה רבה לבא לעזרתם בלב ונפש ולסייע בכל מה דאפשר, וחפץ ה' בידם יצליח לזכות את הדור מזכי הרבים הגדול מאוד, שבודאי זכות כי רב הוא ינן על עם הקודש מכל צרה וצוקה וכו.

וזכות דבר גדול זה וזכות הגאון הק' החפץ חיים זצ"ל ינן עלינו ועל כל ישראל לגאולתן הקרובה בביאת גוא"צ בב"א.

הביד"צ הביד"צ דפעיה"ק ת"ו

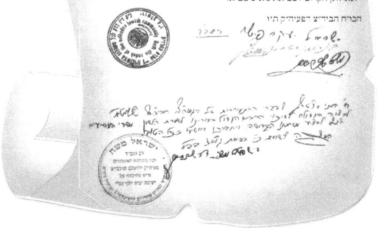

---

* להיות ידוע שהסכמה זו - שניתנה בשעתה להפצת הקונטרסים והקלטות בענין שמיה"ל ואהבת ישראל - היא ההסכמה האחרונה עם חתימת יד קדשו של הגה"צ רבי בנימין ראבינאוויטץ זצ"ל שחתם בליל ר"ח שבט ונסתלק לישיבה של מעלה למחר ביום ר"ח לפני תפלת המוסף. יהא זכרו ברוך.

Jewish Suffering & Tragedy: It's Causes and Preventions

What Every Jew Must Know

PART ONE

Chapter 1: The Power of *Lashon Hara* on a Personal Level
Page 23

Why is the sin of Lashon Hara so severe? / Shmiras Halashon leads to a long and good life. / Shmiras Halashon prevents troubles. / Shmiras Halashon allows us to control the lever of success in our lives.

Chapter 2: The Power of *Lashon Hara* on a National Level
Page 31

The sin of Lashon Hara destroyed the second Bais Hamikdash. / The fast of Tisha B'av primarily relates to the destruction of the third Bais Hamikdash. / This destruction is also due to Lashon Hara. / Lashon Hara is the primary cause of Jewish suffering in the last two millennia. / Lashon Hara is the main reason why the Jewish people are so small in number.

Chapter 3: The Purpose of Creation: Justice and Mercy
Page 39

Hashem created the human soul so that it can share eternity with him. / The dialogue between Hashem and the soul. / The soul must earn its own eternal existence by attaching itself to Hashem through its own free will. / This attachment can only be achieved through the observance of the mitzvos. /. The principle of Justice / Hashem evaluates our performance through the heavenly court of justice. / The heavenly court judges the way we have observed the mitzvos. / The principle of Mercy creates a second court to evaluate our deeds.

Chapter 4: The Power of Guarding One's Speech (Shmiras Halashon)
Page 49

Hashem connects the mouth of the accusing angel to our mouth, so that we can control the judicial process. / A dramatic example to show how our Lashon Hara activates accusations against us. / Hashem advises us not to speak Lashon Hara so as to protect ourselves from the eyes of strict justice. / Various sources indicating this amazing power where we can control the accusations said against us. / The sin of Lashon Hara controls the accusation process which then determines both our personal and national destiny.

Chapter 5: The Tragedy of Our History
Page 59

We are responsible for the suffering and tragedies that befell us. / The reason why Lashon Hara affects the Jews more severely than the gentiles. / The power of the Gentiles lies in their hands. / The power of the Jews lies in their mouths and their prayers. / Lashon Hara damages the Jews only weapon, their mouths and prayers. / The Jews have eroded this power because of their Lashon Hara and their talking in shul.

PART TWO

Chapter 6: The Prohibition of Lashon Hara
Page 67

Definition of Lashon Hara. / The reason why Lashon Hara is prohibited. / The criteria for Lashon Hara. / Circumstances where Lashon Hara is prohibited. / The reason why people speak Lashon Hara.

Chapter 7: The Prohibition of *Rechilus*
Page 81

The difference between Lashon Hara and Rechilus. / The reason why Rechilus is prohibited. / An example of everyday Rechilus.

Chapter 8: How to Stop Lashon Hara and Rechilus
Page 87

The Chofetz Chaim's sensitivity to Rechilus: A Story. / First requirement of Shmiras Halashon: sensitivity to the damage of another person. / Second requirement of Shmiras Halashon: control of which thoughts exit the mouth. / Third requirement of Shmiras Halashon: Knowing the laws of Lashon Hara and Rechilus. / Shmiras Halashon is only difficult in the beginning. / The best motive for Shmiras Halashon: is it worth it?

Chapter 9: The Prohibition of Believing *Lashon Hara* and *Rechilus* (Kabala)
Page 101

The prohibition of listening and believing. / The reason for this prohibition. / It is possible to lie even while telling the truth.

Chapter 10: How to Stop Listening to and Believing in *Lashon Hara* and *Rechilus*
Page 109

Techniques to prevent listening. / Techniques to prevent believing. / Giving other people the benefit of the doubt: a safeguard to believing. / How to give other people the benefit of the doubt.

Chapter 11: When *Lashon Hara* and *Rechilus* Are Permitted
Page 115

Protection as the only reason for permissive Lashon Hara and Rechilus. / The protection overrides against the damage of Lashon Hara and Rechilus. / Lashon Hara and Rechilus are permitted only for minimal and necessary damage. / The 'Protection Override' does not apply to believing Lashon Hara and Rechilus.

Chapter 12: Summary of the Laws
Page 123

Chapter 13:   How to Repent for the Sin of Lashon Hara and Rechilus
Page 127
Undoing the damage caused. / Working on Shmiras Halashon is the best form of repentance. / Arranging a public shiur on the laws of Shmiras Halashon. / Participating in a "Machsom Le'fi" group. / Forgiving people who speak Lashon Hara about yourself. / The spiritual effects of repentance for Lashon Hara and Rechilus.

Chapter 14:   The Truth of Jewish Suffering
Page 131
Shmiras Halashon insures the harmony and survival of the Jewish people even in the face of their transgressions.
/ We have forgotten this profound truth.

Chapter 15:   The Ultimate Challenge for Every Jewish Community
Page 135
Hashem's search for the Lashon Hara-free community. / The necessary action to create the Lashon Hara-free community. / This most fortunate community would lead the Jewish people to their redemption.

PART THREE

Chapter 16:   Our Father, Our King
Page 139
Hashem is a Father when he is merciful and he is a King when he is just. / We always request that Hashem be our Father first and then our King. / The Jewish people can control the dominance of mercy over justice by the way they treat each other. / When Jews ignore each other's dangers, then Hashem acts as a King treating them with strict justice.

Chapter 17:   The Most Powerful Prayer of All
Page 147
A powerful prayer is one that moves Hashem, kviyachol, to become primarily a Father (merciful). / There are three levels

of a prayer's power. / A Jew who is praying only for himself. / A Jew who prays not only for himself but also for another Jew who shares his distress. / A Jew who prays for another Jew because of love only.

Chapter 18: The Obligation to Use the Power Prayer to Redeem Other Jews
Page 153

The power groups are Jews who have a greater power to pray for other Jews. / Two groups of Jews who are in danger are those who are in the process of assimilating and those who live in Israel. / Jews are obligated to pray for each other's welfare. / Ignoring another Jew's danger causes Hashem to become (so to speak) enraged and brings down severe Justice. / When a Jew prays for another Jew he should do so for all endangered Jews without exception.

Chapter 19: The Most Powerful Jewish Community of All
Page 163

DAY 1

PREFACE

Every generation in our history is covered in blood. Why is this so?

When you read any book on Jewish history you become aware of a stark realization. Almost every era, every generation in our history is covered in blood, the blood of countless Jews killed in conquests, pogroms, crusades, inquisitions, and holocausts. Even today in our own time, there are major Jewish communities, notably in Israel, South America, Europe and in the former USSR, who are surrounded by enemies anxiously waiting to drink their blood. In Israel, the continuous occurrences of suicide bombings and the recent shelling of Katyusha rockets from Lebanon in the north and Gaza in the south, where over the course of the past few years hundreds of Jews have been killed or maimed, has made the current climate almost unbearable to live in.

The generation of the biblical King Achav.

But why is this so? Why are we, as a people, so condemned? What do we do to deserve this? The usual answer that is given is that we are being punished because we have sinned, that we have failed to obey the commandments of the Torah in the proper way. If this were the whole truth, however, then we would expect that the sufferings of a generation would be commensurate with its transgressions. The more sins committed, the greater the suffering and tragedy. Yet, we know as a matter of historical fact that this is not so. The generation of the biblical King *Achav* sinned grievously with idolatry, yet they did not suffer greatly[1]. Other generations sinned even less so, yet they suffered much more[2]. If sin is the only factor behind Jewish suffering, then why are there such irregularities? Obviously then, there must be other factors behind Jewish tragedies. What can they be?

Sins are not the only cause of our suffering.

Our *Chazal* have given us the key to solve this problem. They tell us that our sins are not the only cause of our sufferings. Just as damaging is the lack of brotherhood, the lack of peace and the presence of *Lashon Hara* and *Rechilus*[3]. When the Jewish people are united as a family and are at peace with one another, when there is minimal *Lashon Hara* and *Rechilus* amongst them, then sufferings cannot descend upon them even when they deserve them because of their sins. On the other hand, when there is no brotherhood and unity as a family, when there is rampant *Lashon Hara* and *Rechilus*, then all the punishments and sufferings due to them because of their sins tragically befall them.

The absence of Lashon Hara and Rechilus act as a shield that protects the Jewish people.

Clearly, unity as a family, peace, and the absence of *Lashon Hara* and *Rechilus* act as a shield that protects the Jewish people against suffering and tragedy even where there are many sins. But why is this so? What is the underlying truth behind *Chazal*'s teachings? This booklet will answer this question in two parts. Parts one and two will deal with the issue of how the presence of *Lashon Hara* and *Rechilus* causes our sufferings and tragedies. Part three will deal with the issue of how the absence of brotherhood and unity amongst us causes these same results.

We must understand this in order to survive as a people. We have too many enemies waiting to devour us to be ignorant of this critical truth. It is a matter of life and death. Our generation must finally solve this great puzzle and we must do it now. There is no time to lose.

The goal of this booklet.

This booklet has been written to begin this process. It will attempt to clearly explain what our *Chazal* meant. It will present techniques with which to fix these concepts in our minds and incorporate them in our lives. Let it be read by every person who calls himself/herself a Jew. Let it be read and reread until there is a clear light shining in the mind where there was once darkness. Let this information be shared by all Jews who value life and spiritual wellbeing.

This booklet has been written anonymously. It has but one purpose. It is to give the Jewish people a weapon against suffering and tragedy and to bring them closer to their father in Heaven. Let this booklet elevate all Jews so that their heavenly father can have true *nachas* from them. May Hashem, the father, have true joy from the children He loves so dearly.

DAY 2

PART ONE

Chapter One

THE POWER OF *LASHON HARA* ON A PERSONAL LEVEL

Why is the sin of Lashon Hara so severe?

There are 613 mitzvos in the Torah[4]. Some are considered more severe than others[5]. For example, the observance of Shabbos is deemed a very severe obligation (*"chumra d'shabbos"*). We know this from the fact that a Jew who intentionally violates the Shabbos may merit the death penalty according to Torah law. Other sins that are considered to be in the same category of severity include idolatry and homicide. There are other sins, however, that are considered to be in a lesser category since they carry lighter consequences such as *malkos* (lashes) or financial compensation. These include, for example, certain kashrus violations etc[6]. Compared to these lesser categories, the violation of Lashon Hara, slander, against a fellow Jew is considered even less severe in its Torah consequences. It does not incur the death penalty, excision (kores - a shortened life span) or even lashes. Yet, when *Chazal* speak of it, they refer to it in the most severe manner, attributing to its transgressor, the most serious consequences.[7] Why? What makes this commandment so unique amongst all the others?

Shmiras Halashon leads to a long and good life.

The Torah refers to the sin of *Lashon Hara* and the consequences of its restraint in at least two places. Let us examine what it says in each of these places.

1)

מִי הָאִישׁ הֶחָפֵץ חַיִּים אֹהֵב יָמִים לִרְאוֹת טוֹב: נְצֹר לְשׁוֹנְךָ מֵרָע וּשְׂפָתֶיךָ מִדַּבֵּר מִרְמָה:

(תהלים לד, יג-יד)

"Who is the man who desires life, who loves days of seeing good? Guard your tongue from evil and your lips from speaking deceit." (Psalms 34:13-14)

From the first verse we are actually shown two consequences from guarding our speech. From the first part of the verse we see the consequence of life. This literally means a long life. What is considered a long life? It is a life enduring into the eighties and even into the nineties. From the second part of the verse we see the consequence of a good life, a full life with a sound mind and a healthy body. There is no advantage to living a long life if one is sick mentally or physically and therefore requires custodial or constant medical care. The Torah therefore states that guarding one's speech

(Shmiras Halashon) leads to both quantitative (long life) and qualitative (healthy life) blessings.

Shmiras Halashon prevents troubles.

2)
שׁוֹמֵר פִּיו וּלְשׁוֹנוֹ, שׁוֹמֵר מִצָּרוֹת נַפְשׁוֹ: (משלי כא, כג)

"One who guards his mouth and tongue, guards his soul from trouble". (Proverbs 21:23)
From this verse we see a third consequence from guarding our speech. There is a substantial reduction in the aggravations and troubles that life can bring us. We all know the feelings and anguish that troubles can bring. Things we want to accomplish are rarely successful. Stresses we have are often difficult to remove. Yet, the Torah clearly states that what we say about our fellow Jew can have a profound effect on the amount of troubles we will have to encounter.

> From these verses, we clearly see three consequences that directly result from guarding our speech about fellow Jews. They are:
>
> 1) A long life of many years
> 2) A good life where we remain healthy in mind and body and where we are fundamentally, successful in what we do

3) A substantial diminishment of the aggravations and troubles that can potentially afflict us in our lives.

DAY 3

Shmiras Halashon **allows us to control the lever of success in our lives.**

What do these blessings really mean? If we consider the matter, we come to an amazing realization. These three consequences are nothing less than the promise of a successful life. Hashem is actually revealing to us the control lever or button of a successful life! All of us, with all our differences, are actually seeking the same thing -the ability to succeed. Some people want to succeed in their livelihood, others to find an appropriate spouse or, if married, to have children. Still others want to live long and healthy lives. Yet, whatever the goal, we want to succeed in it, to see it actually happen. Is there a way to control this? Can we find some method that truly allows us to succeed, time after time, in whatever we choose to do? From these verses we see that the answer is a resounding YES! Hashem tells us through these verses that the way we speak about a fellow Jew is the single most important factor that determines if we will succeed or fail in our lives. No other commandment in the Torah is connected to such a promise. Even the commandment of honoring one's parents which is connected to the idea of a long life[8] is, nevertheless, not necessarily connected to the idea of a life with few troubles and misfortunes. Only the commandment regarding *Lashon Hara* has such a power to determine the length and quality of our lives.

What does this mean for us? The answer is clear. It means that the way our destiny unfolds is in our hands. After the earthly passing of each person, he or she will have to appear before Hashem, the true judge, and answer for the actions he or she committed in their earthly life. There are those people who will complain to Hashem and ask, "why did I not live such a long life?" To this Hashem will say, "Why do you complain to me. I revealed to you the control lever that determines how long you will live. Why did you not heed it? Why weren't you careful about your Lashon Hara?" There are other people who will bitterly complain, "Why was my life not a good one?" To this Hashem will say, "Why do you complain? You could have made your life much better so that it could be filled with many more successes. You chose however, to ignore the importance of *Lashon Hara* and you suffered the consequences." Finally, there are those who will bitterly complain, "Why was my life so beset with troubles? Why did I have to suffer so much?" To this Hashem will say, "I gave you the power to minimize your sufferings. You have only yourself to blame." A troubling scenario! Clearly then, we will be unable to complain to Hashem since, in truth, we had the power to control and to determine the quantity and quality of our lives.

From everything that has been said until now, we see that the power of speech can enormously influence our personal lives. But where does this power come from? Why is the sin of *Lashon Hara* so unique amongst all the commandments that our *Chazal* warned us so strongly against it? The answer to these questions is critical for only when we truly understand the uniqueness of this commandment will we begin to take it seriously and treat it with the fear and respect that it so richly deserves.

DAY 4

Chapter Two

THE POWER OF *LASHON HARA* ON A NATIONAL LEVEL

The sin of Lashon Hara destroyed the second Bais Hamikdash.

Almost two thousand years ago an enormous tragedy occurred to the Jewish people. The Romans conquered the land of Israel, besieged Jerusalem and destroyed the second Bais Hamikdash. Tens of thousands of Jews were killed or cast into slavery. Jewish sovereignty over the land was terminated. When *Chazal* examined the cause for the divine decree that led to this tragedy, one clear answer loomed in front of them. It was due to the unwarranted and causeless hatred and jealousy that existed between one Jew and his brother (*sinas chinom*)[9]. The Chofetz Chaim in the introduction to his famous book on the laws of *Lashon Hara* makes an important observation about *Chazal's* discovery. He says that the jealousy and enmity that existed in the hearts of the Jews toward each other at that time, by itself, would not have been a sufficient reason to account for such a vast destruction. It was only when those internal negative feelings were actually expressed as Lashon Hara, that is, when the feelings evolved into speech, did the divine decree of destruction become manifest. Thus the primary reason for the destruction of the second Bais Hamikdash and the ensuing exile of the Jews that followed was really because of a very prevalent and continuous pattern of *Lashon Hara* that stemmed from intense feelings of jealousy and baseless hatred[10]. The annual twenty-four hour fast of Tisha B'Av (ninth of Av) was decreed by *Chazal* as a direct consequence of this destruction [11] (and also that of the first Bais Hamikdash as well, since it was destroyed on the same day several centuries earlier[12]). This day was set aside as a day of mourning and fasting.

The fast of Tisha B'av primarily relates to the destruction of the third Bais Hamikdash.

If we consider the matter, however, an important question arises about the annual fast day of Tisha B'Av. Why must the Jews of later generations fast for an event that occurred much earlier in time? They were not there at that time and they were, therefore, not responsible for that tragedy. Moreover, why must they fast every year for the same tragedy? Let one year be sufficient. Why do they need to suffer over nineteen hundred fast days since that time? The answer to this question is startling. In truth, the fast of Tisha B'av has little to do with the destruction of both the first and second Bais Hamikdash. It has everything to do with the destruction of the third Bais Hamikdash! How is this so? Every year since the destruction of the second Bais Hamikdash, Hashem desires to rebuild a third Bais Hamikdash and bring the Jewish people back to their true land, the land of Israel. However, when their deeds are examined, they are seen as unworthy. Accusations are brought against them by the Satan in the heavenly court of Justice and the plans are shelved to be considered the next year. Since the destruction of the second Bais Hamikdash, every generation for every year has, because of their sins, failed to be worthy of rebuilding the third Bais Hamikdash. This failure is considered as an act of destruction since those same sins would have destroyed the Bais Hamikdash had it actually existed[13]. The *Chazal*[14] referred to this notion when they said, "Every generation that fails to rebuild the Bais Hamikdash is considered to have destroyed it." Each generation, on an annual basis, must, therefore, atone and mourn for this loss. The annual fast day of the month of Av, Tisha B' Av, exists primarily to atone for this destruction of the third Bais Hamikdash and only secondarily to mourn for the destruction of the first and second Bais Hamikdash.

DAY 5

This long exile is also due to Lashon Hara.

What are the sins that the Jewish people transgress that are responsible for the annual destruction of the third Bais Hamikdash and their inability to be restored to their land and former elevated position? It is the very same sin that destroyed our last Bais Hamikdash and drove us from our land in the first place. It is the sin of Lashon Hara, the way we feel, treat, and speak about one another, every Jew to his brother. We are still in the shadow of the destruction of the second Bais Hamikdash. We, as a people, have never risen above it. We have failed to cleanse ourselves from this sin and are mired in the same pit as before.

Lashon Hara is the primary cause of Jewish suffering in the last two millennia.

You may think that the sin of *Lashon Hara* is only responsible for the destruction of our second Bais Hamikdash, the exile that followed and the inability to construct the third Bais Hamikdash. This would be a tragic mistake for it doesn't stop there. The sin of unwarranted hatred and jealousy between Jews and the *Lashon Hara* that follows has been a primary cause for every tragedy that the Jews have suffered throughout their long and dark exile of almost two thousand years[15]. The crusades, the Spanish expulsion, the pogroms, the massacres, and even the holocaust itself are all fundamentally connected to the sin of Lashon Hara. It is because of this that our *Chazal* vehemently warned us about the enduring power of this sin over and over again. They were warning us about the fundamental connection between the sin of *Lashon Hara* and Jewish suffering and tragedy. Our greatest folly is that we have failed to grasp this truth and teach it to our children with the same urgency that a mother has when she nurses her child, the necessity of survival itself[16].

The population growth of the Jews in contrast to the Chinese.

You may think at this point that you are truly beginning to grasp the amazing destructive power of *Lashon Hara* as it has affected the Jewish people. This may not be so, not yet. Let me make it clearer by presenting you with a most devastating insight. Historians estimate that about two thousand years ago, during the period of the second Bais Hamikdash, there were approximately six million Jews living throughout the Roman world (including the land of Israel). Historians also estimate that at the same time there were about twenty-four million Chinese in the land of China. Today, there are over a billion Chinese. In contrast, there are only about thirteen million Jews alive in the world today. If two thousand years ago the Jews were one quarter of the total amount of Chinese in the world (an anomaly even then, since the Jews are a much older people and should have been far more numerous), then today they should have a population of at least two hundred and fifty million people (the population size of the United States). Yet, with thirteen million people it means that they have simply doubled in two thousand years whereas the Chinese have increased forty times. The Jews, as one of the oldest people on Earth, should number amongst the largest, yet in reality, they are just about the smallest of all peoples! How could this be? Where did all the Jews go?

Lashon Hara is the main reason why the Jewish people are so small in number.

The answer is devastating. The Jewish people as a nation have experienced throughout their history so many massacres and tragedies that they have been reduced to a dwarf-nation with just about the least number of people on Earth. What caused this? There is only one answer-the destructive power of unwarranted hatred and jealousy as expressed through Lashon Hara. Brotherly jealousy and hatred have left us a mere shadow of our former selves. Instead of becoming a nation whose number can be compared to the stars in heaven or the sands of the sea, we have become a people that can be compared to the trees of a forest-a mere pittance of what we should have been.

There can be no more dramatic reality capable of showing us the power of *Lashon Hara* then that which we have just presented. This reality, however, demands an explanation. What is the nature of this sin, that of Lashon Hara, that enables it to be so destructive? What is the source of its power? How exactly, does it control both our individual and national destinies? In order for us to answer this most important question, however, we must first understand why Hashem created man in the first place and what is his purpose in creation. The answer to this second question will serve as the basis for the answer to the first question.

DAY 6

Chapter Three

THE PURPOSE OF CREATION: JUSTICE AND MERCY

Hashem created the human soul so that it can share eternity with Him.

The Torah reveals to us the extraordinary reason for creation. Hashem desired, because of His absolute goodness, to create another being besides Himself that would resemble Him to the extent that it could, so that it would co-exist with Him for eternity.[17] By experiencing this eternal coexistence, this created being would share with Hashem, to the extent that was possible for it, the reality of the divine. This reality is an ecstatic, joyful existence that knows no diminishment or end. To fulfill this desire, Hashem created the human soul, an extraordinary spiritual essence having an image-like resemblance to Him and fully capable of this experience. At the beginning of its creation, the soul can be said to have entered into a hypothetical dialogue with Hashem, its creator. The dialogue went as follows:

The hypothetical dialogue between Hashem and the soul.

Hashem: "I have created you with the ability to co-exist with me forever and through this I will share the divine experience with you to the extent that it is possible for you. In this circumstance, you will be in constant ecstasy, bathed by the beauty and awe of my divine truth. This will be your world and it is my great gift to you."

Soul: "I am truly staggered by this magnificent gift and the love that is behind it. However, much as it would please me, it also presents certain problems for me. You are the source of existence and consequently, You are the ultimate creator. Since I bear a certain image-like resemblance to you, I have similar creative tendencies. This creator-aspect in me would make me feel very uncomfortable with the idea that my eternal existence is being presented to me as a gift, that is, without my having done anything to create and produce it myself. This discomfort would certainly mar the ecstasy that is your intention for me."[18]

Man has the ability to "create" his own destiny.

Hashem: "I have already foreseen this. The gift that I will give you therefore, will not be the actual eternal existence itself but rather only the possibility for you to create it yourself. You will create it by choosing with your own free will to coexist with Me. Your choice will become your destiny and your final reality, and it will be considered as your act of creation[19]."

Soul: "How and under what circumstances am I to actually make this choice?"

The soul must earn its own eternal existence by attaching itself to Hashem through its own free will.

Hashem: "Your ability to become eternal rests completely with your becoming attached to Me since I and I alone, am the source of all existence. Attachment to Me then, will become the focus of your choice and this choice will affect your ability to exist. However, to enable you to choose freely between attachment and separation from Me, first I must conceal My absolute power and presence from you. This will allow you to have the illusion that you can separate from Me and be completely independent with an existence and power all of your own. With this illusion, you will be able to separate from Me if you so wish.

The physical body and its physical environment.

In order to conceal Myself, I will place you, the soul, temporarily, in a condition where we will no longer be in direct contact. This condition will be a physical world. In this world you will be encased in a body. You will become a human and your body will only allow you to know a reality presented to you from your five senses and nothing more. However, even though I will appear to be hidden from you because of your physicality, it will not be totally so since your intellect and your spiritual sensitivity will allow you to find Me and know of My existence if you seek Me in true humility. Your body, however, will resist this effort by continuously presenting you with impulses and drives in another direction, that of self-empowerment through the pleasure and comforts it offers. Should you choose this direction, we will be separated, and you will lose the ability to co-exist with Me.

This attachment can be achieved only through the observance of the Mitzvos.

To further compel you to choose between attachment or separation from Me once you become human, I will reveal to you certain commandments. Even so, I will still be hidden from you since your body will still separate us. These commandments will apply to your physical being and either direct you to do something (positive commandment) or not to do something (negative commandment). If you listen to your intellect and the intuitive spiritual sense of truth that I have implanted in you, you will realize that I am your creator, your father, and your ultimate destiny. You will be encouraged to observe these commandments and through them you will develop an intimate relationship with Me. This will become your attachment to Me[20].

If, on the other hand you listen to your body and its impulses, you will falsely believe that you can be independent of Me and be a source of your own power. You will then be encouraged to transgress these commandments and because of this become separated from Me. The choice will only be yours and I will not interfere with it. Through that choice, you will either create an eternal co-existence with Me or not.[21] Your ability to create your own destiny by an act of your own free will introduce into the world the principle of Justice. This will become the dominant principle governing your creation and final destiny."

DAY 7

The principle of Justice.

Based on the previous dialogue, it is clear that the possibility of eternal co-existence with the Divine is dependent on our actions and that this fact is the expression of the principle of Justice which states that if we attach to Him, we will exist and if we separate from Him, we will not. The question now is - how does Hashem assess our performance in this matter? How does He judge us to determine our fitness for eternal existence?

Hashem evaluates our performance through the Heavenly Court of Justice.

The Sages tell us that Hashem judges us through a system similar to that on Earth [22], except that it occurs in a spiritual form[23]. The system's central feature is the heavenly court of Justice. In this court Hashem is the judge. The prosecutor or district attorney is an angelic being called the Satan (the word Satan in Hebrew actually means accuser or prosecutor). It is his role to bring before this court all accusations and indictments against all earthly people as to whether they have earned their eternal existence[24]. In opposition to this accusing angel is a defending angel who seeks to defend each person whose case is brought up before this court.

Hashem, the judge, decides the outcome, guilty or innocent, and determines the ensuing judgments.

This court judges the way we have observed the Mitzvos.

This court is the single most powerful entity in all existence. Nothing, absolutely nothing, can affect a person if that court has not ordained it, regardless of the circumstances [25]. In contrast, once something has been ordained, no power in all creation can prevent it since this court represents the power and will of Hashem. Consequently, everything that happens to a person, whether good or bad, is an outgrowth of a decree from this court. Any and every trouble, tragedy, aggravation, or frustration comes only from the decisions of this heavenly court of Justice.

What does this court judge? It judges those actions that we choose to do with our free will. It judges those actions that either attach us or separate us from Hashem, the source of all existence. These actions are the commandments that were revealed to Moshe, by Hashem, at Sinai and written down in the Torah. This court therefore judges whether we have observed or transgressed these commandments. In the final analysis, however, this court judges whether we have earned our eternal existence or not.

The principle of Mercy creates a second court to evaluate our deeds.

Given the fact that the observance of these commandments is the key instrument to achieve eternal existence, Hashem gives us two alternatives. First, He tells us to observe the commandments to the best of our ability. Second, if we fail in this, He tells us that we should repent with as much sincerity as possible since repentance removes the negative effects of sins and rehabilitates a person to his former unsullied status. What happens, however, if a person sins and does not repent so that he doesn't accept either alternative? Can he still be saved from the severe hand of the principle of Justice?

The answer is yes! Hashem has foreseen this possibility and because He loves us so, because He is on our side and wants us to succeed, He has created another court that co-exists simultaneously with that of the court of Justice. This second court judges us as the first one except that it rules according to the principle of Mercy and not that of strict justice. In this second heavenly court of Mercy, even if a person is found guilty, the decrees are much lighter [26].

This court can issue a decree that will postpone any punishment for many years in order to give a person many chances to repent. Even if a punishment is decreed, it can also be staggered over many years, a little bit at a time, making its application much more bearable. Hashem allows the possibility that under certain conditions, this second court of Mercy will adjudicate our sins in place of the court of Justice [27]. In this way, He applies the principle of Mercy [28].

DAY 8

Chapter Four

THE POWER OF GUARDING ONE'S SPEECH (*SHMIRAS HALASHON*)

Hashem connects the mouth of the accusing angel to our mouth so that we can control the judicial process.

If there are two separate and independent courts in heaven co-existing at the same time, one of justice and the other of mercy, under what conditions does Hashem allow the court of Mercy to dominate rather than the court of Justice? When a Jew sins and does not repent, his sins are normally examined in the court of Justice. They are not automatically transferred from the court of Justice to the court of Mercy. How does Hashem decide when to use the principle of Mercy and not that of Justice? The answer to this is simply astonishing. He lets us decide this matter. Each person has the power to choose which court, Justice or Mercy, will oversee his actions. How does this happen?

When a Jew in this world commits a sin, the Satan, the accusing angel and district attorney of this court, first brings up this sin before the heavenly court of Justice. The Satan attempts to present the relevant evidence to gain a conviction. These accusations are actually slanderous remarks (Lashon Hara) about the particular defendant[29]. The Satan, however, is permitted to slander the defendant with his accusations since the principle of Justice requires an evaluation process. Nevertheless, it is still technically considered slander. To give the defendant, however, a better chance to overcome the serious consequences that would result from these accusations, Hashem, in His mercy, initiates an astonishing series of events. He connects the mouth of the accusing angel, the Satan, directly to the mouth of the particular earthly defendant in this matter and upholds the rule of "measure for measure"[30]. If the defendant refrains from slandering (Lashon Hara) a fellow Jew, the Satan cannot open his mouth and slanderously accuse the defendant before the court of Justice. If the defendant, however, does speak Lashon Hara about another Jew, the Satan can then freely begin to accuse the defendant without any hindrance at all[31].

The Satan can only move against a Jew if that Jew moves against another Jew, measure for measure. If Hashem sees that a defendant refrains from Lashon Hara and that the Satan's mouth is closed, He then transfers the accusation immediately to the court of Mercy. In this court, the accusations are not considered slanderous since they are focused on helping the defendant, not punishing him. This remarkable series of events tells us that all accusations are first potentially heard before the court of Justice and that if a Jew so chooses, he can disempower that court and force the accusations to be alternatively heard in the court of Mercy where the judgments affecting him are substantially softened. It is his choice and his choice only and he makes that choice with his mouth and the speech that comes from it. How Hashem must love us, because even when we sin against him, he desires to insulate and protect us from the severity of Justice[32].

A dramatic example to show how our Lashon Hara activates accusations against us.

At this point, you, the reader, may think that you truly begin to grasp the way Lashon Hara can affect your mazal or fortune. This may be true but to ensure that this is so, a crystal-clear analogy will be presented to dramatize the power of your Lashon Hara as it affects the judicial process. At every moment of the day, an angel of Justice appears next to a Jew to observe his actions (of course this angel is completely invisible). Should that Jew commit a sin, the angel prepares to ascend to the heavenly court of Justice to present this information so that he can seek an indictment against that Jew.

Let us be more concrete and call that Jew, Chaim. At every moment, an angel is observing Chaim to see his actions. Suddenly, Chaim decides to eat something that is not kosher. The angel notes the full circumstances surrounding this sin and immediately ascends to heaven. He presents himself before the court of Justice and waits to be called. Moments later, he is summoned and given permission to speak. As he tries to speak, he notices that he is unable to utter any words. He is puzzled. He puts his hand into his pocket and takes a facial mirror from it. He looks into the mirror and to his astonishment, he sees that he has no mouth on his face! He now begins to feel very foolish standing there unable to say a word and he immediately descends to Earth. He finds Chaim and again stands near him to observe. He waits and waits. Suddenly, Chaim begins to speak Lashon Hara against another Jew. The angel begins to feel an itch on his face. He again puts his hand into his pocket and withdraws a facial mirror. He looks into the mirror and behold; a new mouth is forming on his face. He quickly ascends to the heavenly court of Justice and again waits to be summoned. When he is finally called, he says with full conviction, "Chaim has sent me here to accuse him in front of this court. I do so with his full consent!" Other angels then ask him how it is that he can speak against Chaim and even declare that Chaim gave his consent. He answers them as follows. "Had Chaim never spoken Lashon Hara I would never have developed a mouth and without one, I could never have accused him despite the fact that he sinned. Having spoken Lashon Hara, however, Chaim has fully empowered me to speak against him. His sins only gave me the ability to ascend to the heavenly court, but it is his Lashon Hara that empowers me to speak. Shall I then not consider this Chaim's consent?"[33]

    From this scenario we see in a very dramatic way how our Lashon Hara affects the way we are treated from Heaven. It is not only our sins that truly affect us but it is also our speech that has such power. If you were told a story about a person who, while driving, passed a red light and then immediately went to the nearest police station to turn himself in, you would laugh and declare this person to be a fool. If that is so, what can we say about ourselves since we do the very same thing. We first transgress the commandments and then right after that we indulge in Lashon Hara empowering the Satan to report us to the heavenly court of Justice. Are we not fools? Have we not become our own worst enemies?

DAY 9

Hashem advises us not to speak Lashon Hara so as to protect ourselves from the eyes of strict justice.

Given the previous truths, Hashem gives us the following directions. "Do not transgress my commandments because their observance is the basis for your future existence. If, however, you do sin, then immediately repent since this action will erase the negative spiritual energy you created with your sins and restore you to spiritual health. Finally, if you cannot find it in your heart to repent, at least refrain from speaking *Lashon Hara* against your fellow Jew, as this will hide you from the eyes of strict justice and instead entitle you to be judged primarily from the standpoint of compassion and mercy. You will then at least be spared from the grave consequences that emanate from strict justice. Follow these directives and ultimately you will come through. Ignore these directives and you will have only yourselves to blame for the negative results that follow."

Various sources indicating this amazing power where we can control the accusations leveled against us.

How do we know that our speech is so powerful that it can directly affect the quality of our lives?

In the Talmud Yerushalmi,[34] it states that in the time of King *Achav*, even though that generation worshipped idols[35], nevertheless, their wars were victorious because they refrained from speaking Lashon Hara. In the time of the king Saul however, even though there was much less idolatry and even considerable Torah scholarship[36], nevertheless, because of that generation's prevalent *Lashon Hara* they lost the wars they undertook[37]. From this Yerushalmi, we see that it was the sin of *Lashon Hara* that was primarily responsible for the victories or defeats of those generations[38]. Other sins did not affect the outcomes as much. Moreover, we see the astonishing fact that even in the presence of that generation's rampant idolatry (in King *Achav*'s time), the greatest sin of all, guarding their speech still had the power to grant successes and shower them with mercy.

The *Midrash* in *Yalkut Shimoni*[39] it states the following. "The Holy One, blessed be He, says, from all the tragedies that come upon you, I can save you, but from those that come through Lashon Hara, hide yourself as best as you can since from them, I cannot save you." Again, we clearly see the destructive power of *Lashon Hara* because in its presence, the doors of mercy are closed and, so to speak, we are on our own. However, in the absence of Lashon Hara, Hashem declares His total willingness to save us from any troubles. This results from moving ourselves and our sins to the heavenly court of Mercy since we refrained from any Lashon Hara.

One of the most poignant references to the fact that the *Lashon Hara* spoken between Jews empowers the Satan to accuse them in front of the heavenly court of Justice is found in the Zohar. **The Zohar[40] states** explicitly that only through the sin of *Lashon Hara* can the Jews awaken the examination process of Justice against them. It states: ***"The awakening of Justice from above (Heaven) is completely conditional upon the awakening of Justice from below (Earth) through Lashon Hara. The consequence of this awakening brings the sword and death to the world."*** There are many other references about this issue stated in the commentaries[41]. A summary of them can be found in the *sefer Shmiras Halashon* (*Sha'ar HaZechirah*, chapters two and four) by the Chofetz Chaim.

The sin of Lashon Hara controls the accusation process which then determines both our personal and national destiny.

If we truly grasp the meaning of everything we have stated thus far, we can begin to answer the central question that we asked before, namely, why *Lashon Hara* as a sin is so powerful that it controls our personal and national destinies. It controls our personal destiny, that is the length of our life, its quality, and the troubles we experience because it determines if these aspects will be dominated by the principle of Justice or by the principle of Mercy. The presence of *Lashon Hara* in our speech arouses the principle of Justice and causes it to dominate. The absence of *Lashon Hara* in our speech arouses the principle of Mercy and causes it to dominate. *Lashon Hara* therefore acts like a switch. If a person refrains from speaking Lashon Hara, even if he sins, his life will be long, good and relatively free of troubles because having aroused Mercy, it will always come to his defense and shed the best possible light on him. If a person speaks Lashon Hara, then his sins will be held against him. His life will not be so long, good or free of troubles since having aroused Justice, it will always pursue him with grave consequences.

The same concept applies equally to our national destiny as a people. This is why our *Chazal* warned us so emphatically against unwarranted hatred and the *Lashon Hara* that results. They are telling us what is perhaps one of the most important concepts in the Torah as far as Jewish destiny is concerned. It is that the sins of the Jews mean only that they must eventually be judged. But how they are judged whether through strict justice or mercy is determined mainly by their speech about each other, that is, whether there is the presence or absence of *Lashon Hara* in it. The way they are judged can make all the difference between their salvation or their suffering.

DAY 10

Chapter Five

THE TRAGEDY OF OUR HISTORY

We are responsible for the suffering and tragedies that befell us.

What dawns on us at this point is a thought so terrifying that it should cause us to shake and tremble. The tragedies and catastrophes of the last two thousand years didn't have to happen! The blood and gore that fills the pages of Jewish history could have been prevented or at least substantially diminished. If we as a people had truly grasped what our *Chazal* saw so clearly back then and if we had only taken their admonitions seriously, then how many Jewish lives could have been saved. If we had only realized that it is the way that we are judged, either with strict justice or with mercy, and not the fact that we are judged that is responsible for our tragedies, then how much Jewish suffering could have been averted.

Woe unto us as a people for having ignored the prescriptions of our spiritual advisors and instead followed our own ineffective remedies. We have betrayed ourselves because we have ignored the voice of Hashem speaking out to us in every generation saying, "Hear Me, My children. I can save you from your sins even though I must judge them because I have great compassion and mercy, but this is only so if you do not oppose it. Desist from your jealousies, conflicts, hatreds and *Lashon Hara* and I will silence all of your accusers and protect you under My wings. My great mercy is yours to take. Don't turn it away!"

The reason why Lashon Hara affects the Jews more severely than the gentiles.

At this point you may ask a very important question. If the *Lashon Hara* of the Jews is so damaging, what about the *Lashon Hara* of the non-Jews, since they speak just as much, if not more of it? Why doesn't their *Lashon Hara* have the same damaging effect on their destiny? Specifically, in the comparison with the Chinese cited before, why have the Chinese been able to override the damage of their *Lashon Hara* and produced a population of over a billion people whereas the Jews were unable to do so and they thereby diminished their numbers to a fraction of what they should have been?

The answer to this question points to the amazing spiritual level of the Jews in contrast to all the other peoples of the world. When Yitzchok Avinu blessed Yaakov, he said "the voice is the voice of Yaakov (it sounded like Yaakov's voice) but the hands are the hands of Eisav (he felt like Eisav to the touch)"[42]. On the simple level, Yitzchok was confused as to the identity of the son who was before him.

The power of the Gentiles lies in their hands.

On a deeper level, Yitzchok Avinu was saying something very profound. He was describing the essential difference between Yaakov's descendants, the Jews, and Eisav's descendants, the gentiles. He was describing their power centers. In order for the gentiles to succeed in the physical world, they must use their hands, that is, they must do something physically. In order for the Jews to succeed in the physical world, they must use their voice, that is, they can rely on simply saying something, meaning, they can rely on their prayers to Hashem and He will enable them to succeed by his direct intervention into physical reality[43].

The power of the Jews lies in their mouths and their prayers.

When the gentiles want to succeed at war, they must use the brute force of their hands or use physical technology. The Jews, because of the power of their mouth, can utter a series of prayers and vanquish the enemy through Hashem's intervention. There are many examples of this ability as seen in the battle of Gideon [44] and in the battle of King Chizkiyah against the Assyrians when they surrounded Jerusalem[45]. King David clearly points to this ability when he says: *"These rely upon chariots and these rely upon horses but we - in the name of Hashem, our G-d, we call out. They slumped and fell, but we arose and were invigorated"*[46]. The unique ability of the Jews to stir reality with the power of their mouths and prayers as opposed to their hands alludes to their extraordinary spiritual elevation. This is why the Torah obligates them for 613 commandments. The gentiles, who must rely on actual physical intervention by their hands are not so elevated and are therefore only obligated to the seven commandments of the sons of Noach.

DAY 11

Lashon Hara damages the Jews only weapon: their mouths and prayers.

The ability of the Jews to employ the power of the mouth is an exalted one but nevertheless, it is also a precarious one since it can easily be compromised and damaged. It can be damaged by indulging in the prohibitive actions regarding the mouth, *Lashon Hara* and *Rechilus*, which can contaminate this instrument and render it ineffective.

The fact is that *Lashon Hara* is a two-edged sword and is thus very dangerous for the Jews. It empowers the Satan to accuse them in the heavenly court of Justice and produce from these accusations serious consequences in the form of decrees that can affect their destiny. This is one edge of the sword. The other edge of the sword is that *Lashon Hara* diminishes and erodes the power center of the Jews, their mouths, and prayers, thereby preventing them from protecting themselves from the very selfsame accusations of The Satan that they previously empowered. Gradually, the ensuing decrees from the heavenly court of Justice descend upon them because their prayers are now very weak[47]. They are trapped in a vise constructed by their own speech. They become vulnerable and can eventually be victimized by all the gentile nations of the world, even the lowest among them.

Chazal warned us not to erode our power center through Lashon Hara.

Chazal clearly knew this and warned us during the destruction of the second Bais Hamikdash. They understood that the Jews were eroding their power center through *Lashon Hara* and that once lost, they would be at the mercy of their numerous enemies for the rest of their history. Even more ominously, they knew that this loss could not be compensated because the Jews could not usurp from the gentiles the power of the hands since it was never their entitlement to begin with. Without the power of the mouth and without the power of the hands, the Jews would have nothing. The result is two thousand years of blood-soaked history.

The gentiles can retain their power even while indulging in Lashon Hara.

The gentiles are also damaged by their Lashon Hara. However, since their power center lies in their hands and not in their mouths, their main power is not affected and the damage to their mouths is considered only secondary. That is why, despite their Lashon Hara, the Chinese can proliferate to a population of a billion people. That is why every gentile nation is more powerful than a Jewish nation that indulges in *Lashon Hara* because at least they retain the power of their hands while the Jews lose everything.

The Jews have eroded this power because of their Lashon Hara and their talking in shul.

The erosion of the power of the Jews continues until this very day. There are two reasons for this. Firstly, we are still sadly engrossed in the sin of Lashon Hara. Our mouths and our prayers cannot be truly repaired until this sin is gradually eliminated or at least reduced. Secondly, our attitude about our shuls and our activities therein undermines us in a powerful way[48]. There is simply too much idle talk in shul at the time of prayer and this erodes our power center substantially.

The Shuls are our arsenal headquarters and central command stations.

If the power of the Jews is in their mouths and prayers, then their synagogues and houses of worship are their arsenal headquarters and central command stations. It is an absolute truth before Hashem, that the power of a synagogue at the time of prayer is greater than the power of the nuclear arsenals of the gentile nations. This seems incredible but everything in the Torah's viewpoints to this conclusion. The power of Hashem is greater than anything and that which evokes this power is the most powerful instrument of all, without exception. Since the Jews, through their prayers, excel in this ability, their power is superior to all others. Given this truth, what should be their behavior in their synagogues at the time of prayer?

Clearly it should be with the greatest respect and dignity considering the power that their prayers have to influence reality.

Proper behavior in Shul at the time of prayer.

What actually occurs? There is a great deal of talking and incessant chatter and many times it is actually Lashon Hara[49]. We have all seen rabbis plead with their congregations to remain quiet. The spiritual damage to the Jews because of this is incalculable[50]. What must Hashem see in such cases? He sees a people who were given the greatest power of all, yet sadly he sees them disregard this gift and even trample upon it. He sees a blind people unable to see that, from their mouths, ensue the mightiest forces of existence, forces far greater than that which can proceed from the armaments of all the nations of the world. When will we learn? When will we purify our mouths and become once again the nation Hashem intended us to be, a spiritually clean and holy people capable of moving Heaven and Earth with the mere breath of our mouths?

DAY 12

PART TWO

Note: *The following overview has been written with the intent to give the reader an outline and a general feel of the complex laws of Shmiras Halashon. However, one should not use this as a guide for practical Halachah. This would necessitate a far more thorough and extensive treatment of these Halachos, which is beyond the scope of this work. Therefore, one should consult the Sefer Chofetz Chaim or a competent halachic authority before applying the halacha practically.*

Chapter Six

THE PROHIBITION OF *LASHON HARA*

The definition of Lashon Hara

What precisely is Lashon Hara? It refers to any revelation of information that one can anticipate will possibly lead to hurting or damaging the well-being of another Jew in any sense, physically, emotionally, socially or economically[51]. This revelation usually takes the form of speech, but it can also be expressed through writing[52] or even body gestures and facial expressions[53], since any of these methods can **reveal information** that can damage another[54]. It does not matter if the information revealed is completely true or completely false[55]. It is strictly forbidden to relate it in either case. Where the information, however, is false, it is considered much worse and is distinguished by its own term *"motzei shem ra"*[56]. The truth or the falsity of the information revealed is not the issue in the prohibition. The central governing principle in determining *Lashon Hara* is whether the revelation can be anticipated to do damage.

The reason why Lashon Hara is prohibited

At this point you may argue the following. As long as a person sticks to the absolute truth, why should such a revelation be prohibited? In fact, the secular, gentile courts agree with this argument. If you slander someone and are sued in a secular court of law, then as long as you can prove your slanderous remarks to be true, you can be exonerated. Why is the Torah's view different?

People are sensitive not to reveal information that can potentially damage a family member.

The answer to this question is subtle and somewhat unexpected. If you knew a terrible secret about a family member, you would never reveal this to anyone in idle conversation because it might hurt this person. You would be sensitive to that hurt since it involves a loved one, a family member. In such a case, the potential damage to this person far outweighs the desire to reveal this truth in a conversation. Clearly, regarding your family, the truth does not matter, causing hurt and damage does. But if you knew a truth about another Jew, one who was not close to you at all, chances are that you would reveal it even if that revelation would hurt and damage that Jew. Why? Because that Jew in your eyes is like a stranger and in this case, the desire to reveal this truth of that person in a conversation outweighs any possible damage that could result from that revelation.

In the eyes of Hashem, so to speak, all Jews are related and considered as one family.

In Hashem's eyes, however, you would be damaging a brother or a sister, not a stranger[57]. In the eyes of Hashem, so to speak, all Jews are related and considered as a family since He is the creator and father of them all. There are no strangers amongst Jews in Hashem's eyes no matter how distant they are from each other[58]. Your actual brother and sister remain such even if many oceans separate them from you. So too it is with all Jews-they are forever one family. This, then, is the answer to our question. Truth doesn't matter, family does and since all Jews are family, we cannot hurt them, even with the truth. *Lashon Hara* is therefore forbidden for all Jews in spite of the fact that it is completely true.

Possession of a truth is not our entitlement to reveal it.

We all suffer from a common misconception. We think that just because we know certain things about fellow Jews, because they are true, we have the right to reveal them. It is as if we were some kind of self-appointed reporter for the local newspaper and that the possession of a truth is its own entitlement to reveal it. We must learn that this is very wrong. Just because we know something does not mean we have the right to reveal it. We must consider its damage potential as well as its truth since every conversation about a fellow Jew is always a conversation about a family member.

DAY 13

The criteria for Lashon Hara: potential damage, loss of respect and embarrassment

How do we know when we have spoken *Lashon Hara*? We must ask ourselves three questions before we reveal something about a fellow Jew:

1) **Damage.** If I reveal this information, can I anticipate that it could in some way cause some kind of hurt or damage to a fellow Jew? If the answer is yes, it is considered *Lashon Hara*[51]. This damage goes beyond simple slander or defamation of character. It applies to any type of damage. Moreover, someone can be hurt even if his name is not mentioned in a conversation[60]. For example, if someone is told a business fact in confidence and then he reveals it to a third party knowing that a possible hurt can ensue for the person who revealed it to him, it is considered *Lashon Hara* even where no name is mentioned at all [61].

   Most people mistakenly believe that *Lashon Hara* refers only to slanderous and defamatory remarks about someone. This is untrue. It refers to any revelation that has the potential to damage and where the revealer can anticipate this possibility[62]. Even if the potential damage never actually occurs, the sin is nevertheless there because the prohibition of *Lashon Hara* applies even to the attempt and not only to the actual occurrence of damage[63].

2) **Loss of Respect.** If I reveal this information, can I anticipate that the person listening to me will, as a result, begin to devalue and look down upon the person I am talking about? If the answer is yes, it is considered *Lashon Hara*[64]. This is true even where most people would not devalue someone based on this information. If my listener will, it is *Lashon Hara*. Even if the devaluation or loss of respect is minimal, it is *Lashon Hara*. If it is substantial, then the speaker is in big trouble, spiritually[65].

3) **Embarrassment.** If I reveal this information about someone and were he able to overhear what I am about to say, would he feel embarrassed and humiliated? If the answer is yes, it is considered Lashon Hara[66].

If you are in doubt about the possible outcome, it is better not to say anything.

The answers to all of these questions are clearly based on the speaker's judgment about his impending revelations. If he is concerned about his *mazal*, he must be very careful about his decisions. Should he make a mistake and reveal the information innocently thinking that it would not have a negative effect, he can be exonerated[67]. But if he didn't even think about these issues, that is another matter. If he is in doubt about the possible outcome, it is better not to say anything[68]. Why risk the serious consequences of *Lashon Hara* for himself. The rule is, when in doubt, don't. It is important to realize that not all the answers to these three questions need to be in the affirmative for a revelation to be *Lashon Hara*. Even if only one of these questions is answered in the affirmative and the others are not, it is still considered *Lashon Hara*. Thus, for example, where a revelation does not cause a listener to devalue the subject, nevertheless, if it can be anticipated that the subject would be embarrassed if he could overhear it, it is still *Lashon Hara*.

Circumstances where Lashon Hara is prohibited.

It is clear that the central principle governing the Torah's prohibition of *Lashon Hara* is the concept of damage, that is, a revelation's ability to potentially damage a victim either in a general way or in regard to his reputation (slander). Because of this, it doesn't make any difference whether the revelation:

- was true or false ("veracity of information").
- was communicated through a verbal statement, written document or body sign ("mode of communication").

- was volunteered or said in response to a question ("manner of elicitation") [69].
- explicitly contained the person's name or not. If the listener can figure out who is being talked about on his own, it is *Lashon Hara.* ("Subject identification")[70].
- was motivated through jealousy[71], revenge[72], the desire to gain approval and recognition[73] or was simply said as a joke[74]. ("Motivation"). The Torah does permit one motivation, however, as a valid reason to speak Lashon Hara. It is the need to protect someone. More on this protection motive later. (See Chapter 11 "When are *Lashon Hara* & *Rechilus* permitted?").
- was communicated because of some pressure[75] or incentive, such as to prevent a financial loss[76], to prevent a loss of honor[77], to gain a profit[78], or even to honor a parent or rabbi[79]. Just as the laws of kashruth cannot be compromised because of these reasons, so too the laws of Lashon Hara. ("Incentive").
- was about someone's religious behavior[80], personality[81], intelligence[82], abilities[83], health[84], property[85], finances[86] or family[87]. If it can potentially cause damage to this person, it is *Lashon Hara.* ("Content").
- was communicated to a spouse[87], relative[88], friend or stranger. Even one's spouse can, by listening, devalue a person thereby causing damage to that person's reputation. ("Recipient").

- o was communicated to an adult or even to a child[89].
- o was about a child[90], adult, stranger, friend or even a spouse[91]. Marriage does not create an entitlement to hurt your spouse by speaking *Lashon Hara*. ("Subject").

Lashon Hara about non-Jews.

A question that is often asked is whether *Lashon Hara* is permitted to be spoken against a non-Jew. The answer to this is subtle. The Torah clearly prohibits *Lashon Hara* against another Jew from a halachic or legal standpoint[92]. A non-Jew, however, does not share this same status. Even so, it is unadvisable to speak *Lashon Hara* against a non-Jew when it is unwarranted, for ethical and moral reasons. We are required as Jews, to treat a righteous gentile in an ethical way[93].

DAY 14

The reason why people speak Lashon Hara.

Why do people speak Lashon Hara? What are the usual motives for doing so? There are three major reasons which cause people to indulge in Lashon Hara: Jealousy, revenge, and the desire for approval. Let us examine each one in turn.

Jealousy. Any society which sponsors material success as the main way to enhance self-esteem is going to find that jealousy will be very prevalent. If money, possessions, and position become the key symbols to success and social status, then people who have not acquired these things will be very jealous of people who have. Competition and self-centeredness will become the rule, while sharing and charitable concerns will become the exception. A lack of material things will breed self-doubt and threaten self-esteem. This in turn will arouse jealousy which will then find expression as unwarranted hatred and Lashon Hara.

Revenge. A second major cause of *Lashon Hara* is revenge. People who feel slighted and hurt by another's actions or words will harbor resentment and animosity towards that person. Eventually, these feelings will spill over, and the injured person will satisfy himself with the expression of Lashon Hara.

Social Acceptance. The third cause is the need for approval, that is, to be liked and to be socially accepted. This will motivate a person to become a source of information and gossip about people so that other people will be attracted to him since most people enjoy hearing the "latest" about others.

In all of these motivations, *Lashon Hara* becomes a very useful instrument to raise a lowered sense of self-esteem that a person unconsciously feels about himself. But look at the consequences! He may be feeling better about himself but at what cost. An accusing angel is suddenly empowered to attack him in front of the heavenly court of Justice, potentially causing serious damage to his *mazal* and fortune. Is it worth it!

The credit card analogy.

Speaking *Lashon Hara* is in certain ways similar to using a credit card. You go into a store and see an item, say a piece of furniture that you wish to buy. You ask the salesperson how much it is, and he says, "don't worry, just give me your credit card." You give him your credit card and feel relieved; it was so easy. You forget about the purchase until you receive the credit card bill a month later. You see the price of $500 for the furniture. You feel disturbed. It is so much money, but it felt so easy when you used a credit card and now, when the bill arrives, it feels so painful.

Was it worth it?

Lashon Hara produces the same type of experience. It is so easy to speak it[94]. Like a credit card, it appears as if nothing has happened. Words cannot be seen, so what did you do? Later in time, difficulties begin to appear in your life that should not be, that make no sense. Your fortune begins to change, and you cannot understand why. The truth is that the *Lashon Hara* bill has arrived and it is time to pay. Now it feels very painful. Your accusing angels are now having their day. Was it worth it?

DAY 15

Chapter Seven

THE PROHIBITION OF *RECHILUS*

The definition of Rechilus.

Just as the Torah prohibits Lashon Hara, so too it prohibits *Rechilus* (tale-bearing)[95]. What is the difference between the two? When a person speaks Lashon Hara, he reveals information that can create damage for someone. When he speaks *Rechilus*, he reveals information that can cause two Jews to become enemies or to simply become hostile and angry at each other. *Rechilus* is therefore the revelation of certain information to a listener ("recipient") causing him to feel that he (or a close family member[96]) has been adversely affected by another Jew, which then creates an animosity between him and that other person[97]. *Rechilus* is actually a special case of *Lashon Hara* since by causing hostility between two Jews you damage their relationship. It is, however, a distinct prohibition due to its special power to create hostility.

The different effects of Lashon Hara and Rechilus.

The effects of *Lashon Hara* and *Rechilus* can be quite different. For example, if someone tells you in idle conversation that Chaim (a person you both know) is a very selfish man, this is Lashon Hara. Your reaction, if you believe it, would possibly be to lose respect for Chaim and no longer associate with him socially. Lashon Hara, by fostering loss of respect, prevents or destroys friendships. However, if someone tells you that Chaim told him that you were a very selfish person, this is *Rechilus*. Your reaction would be much stronger. Not only would you possibly cut off from Chaim socially, but chances are that you would be so furious with him that you could even become his enemy[97].

Rechilus can cause two Jews to become enemies with each other.

Rechilus, by fostering hostility, can actually create enemies[98]. You would be speaking *Rechilus* if you revealed to a listener certain negative remarks or actions that someone said about him or did to him (or to anyone close to him such as family or friends) and because of this he could become angry at the person who said those remarks or did those things.

The reason why Rechilus is prohibited.

But what is wrong with *Rechilus*? The prohibition of *Lashon Hara* is understandable since you are being told someone else's flaws. But if you are told someone's negative opinion about you, don't you have a right to know? Don't you have a right to know who is your true friend and who is not? Why should the Torah prohibit such information?

Unbridled Rechilus would destroy the brotherhood of the Jewish people.

The answer is surprising. It is a common occurrence that when people are in a bad or sullen mood, they say negative things about other people. In such a mood, it is possible for husbands and wives, brothers and sisters, friends, and acquaintances, to make disparaging remarks about each other to third parties. Certainly, however, they do not want the people they are talking about to know about these comments from these third parties because it could jeopardize their relationship with them. They are just venting or complaining, a common human trait, and do not really mean what they say. Because of this, the Torah does not want people to know the negative remarks said about them unless they need this information to protect themselves.

The Torah feels that if a person were always told the negative remarks that other people were saying about him under all circumstances, he would not have a friend or relationship left in the world because of the resentment he would develop toward these people. Unbridled *Rechilus* would therefore make everyone into enemies and destroy the brotherhood of the Jewish people[99]. That is one of the main reasons why *Rechilus* is forbidden.

An example of everyday Rechilus.

Let us give an example where even innocent remarks can be considered *Rechilus* or *Avak Rechilus*.

> *Sarah met her sister-in-law Miriam at the shopping mall. Miriam was carrying many packages and Sarah commented about that. Miriam explained that she had had a great day shopping, buying many things on sale, on clearance, and at great discounts. Sarah bid Miriam farewell and, on her way home, met her brother Reuven, Miriam's husband. Sarah then told him of her meeting with Miriam at the mall. Suddenly, Reuven became very angry at his wife for her extravagant shopping spree. Sarah painfully realized that her revelation incited her brother (Miriam's husband) to become angry at his wife. She realized that she had just spoken Rechilus even though her remarks were not negative because she could have anticipated that since many marriages have money issues, possibly so does that of Miriam and Reuven. She understood that as innocent as her revelation was, she should have thought of their possible repercussions first.* 100

The prohibition of *Rechilus* tells us that not everything that a person knows, or experiences should be revealed because not every person has a right to know these things since it can create hostility. Even if the information does not directly affect the listener adversely and therefore it is not considered *Rechilus*, you should still be careful before you reveal it if you can anticipate that it can create jealousy and hostility[101].

For example, if you have a friend who is going on a five-week vacation to Europe or Eretz Yisroel, should you spread this news around to common friends? Do these other people need to know this information? If it may make them jealous and incite them to speak Lashon Hara, then of course it is better that they do not know. Again, just because you know something doesn't mean you should reveal and share it. Beware of the possibility of creating jealousy and hostility even where no *Rechilus* is involved.

DAY 16

Chapter Eight

HOW TO STOP *LASHON HARA* AND *RECHILUS*

How can we control an action that is usually done without much thought?

At this point, you have a fairly clear idea of the power of *Lashon Hara* and *Rechilus* and the damage that they can do to you. You also know some of the key concepts attached to these prohibitions. But how do you control them? Talking is as natural as breathing. How can we control an action that is so effortless and is usually done without much thought? The truth is that controlling *Lashon Hara* and *Rechilus* is not as difficult as you might think. The major difficulties exist only at the outset[102] and after a while they gradually disappear, leaving you very much in control of your speech[103]. There are several steps to be taken to become a master of your speech. Let us examine them in detail.

The Chofetz Chaim's sensitivity to Rechilus: A Story.

There is a very interesting story told by Rav Shalom Schwadron, ZT'L, about the saintly Chofetz Chaim, ZT'L[104]. The Chofetz Chaim (he was called this name after the title of his famous book on the laws of Lashon Hara) and another distinguished Rav[105] were once traveling on the road somewhere in Poland with the purpose of performing a mitzva. On the way, they stopped at an inn known for its high standards of kashruth. The owner instantly recognized them and took their order. After the meal was finished, the owner asked the rabbis if they enjoyed their meal. The Chofetz Chaim replied that the meal was very satisfactory. The other rav replied that while the meal was good, nevertheless, it lacked enough salt so that it was not truly satisfying. Thereupon the owner departed and went into the kitchen.

The Chofetz Chaim suddenly turned to his companion and criticized him saying that his remarks were prohibited since they contained *Rechilus* and Lashon Hara. He explained that as a result of his reply, the owner probably felt disturbed since he wanted to please them. He further stated that, probably, at this very moment, the owner was censuring the cook and that since this position was usually filled by a poor widow, she was probably crying in fear of losing her job. The other Rav objected to this criticism and claimed that it was an exaggeration since his remark was simply an observation about the saltiness of the food.

The Chofetz Chaim arose and took the other Rav into the kitchen. When he opened the kitchen door, they saw the exact scene that the Chofetz Chaim had predicted. The owner was censuring the cook, a poor widow, who was crying profusely and begging to remain at her job. Immediately, the shocked Rav attempted to intervene and intercede on behalf of the cook so that no harm would result from his remarks.

The first requirement of Shmiras Halashon: sensitivity to the damage of another person.

When we analyze this story, an interesting question arises. How did the Chofetz Chaim know, in advance, what would ensue from the other rabbi's remarks? The answer lies at the heart of the control of *Lashon Hara* and *Rechilus*. He knew intuitively that a comment about the saltiness of the food was, in its essence, a comment about the competence of the cook and that the owner's disappointment could easily translate itself into hostility towards the cook thereby threatening her employment. His perception of the situation was an outgrowth of a highly developed sensitivity to feel, in advance, potentially threatening situations for other people. He developed in himself a heightened awareness for the feelings of other people and how they can be affected by the events surrounding them, especially ominous ones.

When it comes to other people our sensitivities are dulled.

All of us have long ago developed this sense for ourselves. For example, we know that if there is ice on the road, we must walk slowly and not run. We do not need a sign or another person to tell us of its dangers. Even in subtle situations, we can distinguish almost immediately between those events that will support us and those events that will threaten us. We can also frequently distinguish between a person who is a friend and one who is a foe from only a remark, a facial expression, or a voice intonation. When it comes to other people, however, we are only attuned to obviously threatening circumstances such as when another person runs quickly into the street without looking for oncoming cars. But in subtle situations, our sensitivities are dulled, and we are unable to predict, in advance, potentially damaging consequences for other people, especially strangers.

Shmiras Halashon requires a clear recognition of another person's existence.

The Chofetz Chaim saw other people, friends, and strangers, as he saw himself. He truly fulfilled the commandment, "and you shall love your neighbor as yourself." With this quality, he was able to effectively guard himself from hurting others during daily conversation[106].

Why can't we do this? Why don't we possess this quality? The answer is that, unfortunately, most of us are too self-centered and wholly focused on our own successes and failures. Other people come into our focus only when they relate to our needs and expectations.

Otherwise, they are like mere blips on our radar screens and are not to be taken seriously. Guarding one's *Lashon Hara* successfully, requires a clear recognition of another person's existence beyond our own and a sensitivity to his feelings and to what may harm him[107].

DAY 17

The second requirement of Shmiras Halashon: The control of which thoughts exit the mouth.

Is the possession of this sensitivity enough to guard against *Lashon Hara*? The answer is no. From the time that we were small, we have said whatever we have thought. Our thoughts were never evaluated before they were said. As soon as they entered our mind, they always had full license to exit our mouth. It's as though there was a special pipe connecting the brain to the mouth. As soon as the thoughts entered one end, it quickly flew out of the other end as speech. We have, out of habit, lost control of our speech. Without this control, there is no way we can guard our tongue from emitting harmful words. To guard our speech, we must take this control back. One cannot evaluate his speech if it flies by too quickly.

Gaining control of our speech: a technique.

How do we do this? There is a very simple exercise that, in a short time, can quickly restore a person to this control. Every day in your regular conversations with other people, select a specific thought and withhold it from being spoken. The thought may be a fact, an opinion, a novel idea, and may be fully permissible to say. Nevertheless, arbitrarily select this thought and stop yourself from expressing it telling yourself that it is you who are in control of your mouth and that you and not your mouth will decide what will be said and what will not be said. Practice this exercise selecting three thoughts from the hundreds of thoughts that come to mind during the day.

After a while you will notice that something strange is happening. Your thoughts, as they enter your mind, will begin to diminish their speed to your mouth and no longer automatically flow out into your speech. In a short while they will actually stop, and it will feel like they are sitting in your head waiting for your approval on whether or not to be expressed. Suddenly you will realize that you are truly in charge. For perhaps the first time, you can begin to evaluate your thoughts before you spill them out and it is too late. You can evaluate them because now you can first listen to them. They are now yours to control[108].

The third requirement of Shmiras Halashon:
Knowing the laws.

Is the possession of the sensitivity to the damage of other people along with the ability to screen your thoughts enough to enable you to guard your tongue? The answer is not yet. There is yet one more important element that you will need to have before you can succeed. You will need to know how to evaluate your potential speech, that is, to know what factors and which situations make your communications permissible or prohibited. You will need to be familiar with the laws of *Lashon Hara* and *Rechilus*[109].

Damaging words are invisible and show no clear sign that they are forbidden.

The necessity to know the laws is especially true with respect to the commandment of guarding your tongue. If someone were to place a piece of meat on a plate before you and invite you to eat it, certainly, you would first attempt to identify the meat to see if it was kosher. If you saw that it was pork, you would immediately push it away and refuse to eat it. This would be very easy since the prohibited substance is clearly recognizable to your senses.

In the case of Lashon Hara, this would be much more difficult. The prohibited substance, the damaging words coming from your mouth, are invisible and show no clear sign to your senses that they are forbidden. You could only identify these spiritually poisonous words by a clear knowledge of the laws that describe them. Here, knowledge of the laws would replace knowledge of the senses. It is only after you possess this third element that you will be in a position to completely master your speech and guard your tongue from speaking *Lashon Hara* and *Rechilus*.

DAY 18

Shmiras Halashon is only difficult at the beginning.

At this point, many people will begin to complain as follows. "Even if I develop a sensitivity to other people's hurt and I learn how to evaluate my own thoughts before I say them according to the laws of Lashon Hara, nevertheless, it will still require a tremendous effort not to speak Lashon Hara. It would require an enormous and continuous conscious effort on my part that would then result in my conversation losing its natural and easy flow. How can Hashem expect me to do this? It seems that the only way to comply is to almost stop talking altogether[110]. This too would be unnatural and very unrealistic" [111].

The answer to this question is very important to know because it involves a principle that not only applies to the process of guarding one's speech, but it also applies to the process behind all spiritual growth. In the beginning of any self-control process, without question, a certain amount of conscious effort is required. After a short while, however, this conscious effort becomes less demanding and gradually it is replaced by an effortless, intuitive sense[112].

In other words, what starts out as a process of conscious deliberation eventually ends as a process that is automatic and almost instinctive. This was already seen in the process described earlier where we tried to control the automatic flow of thoughts into speech. The beginning of the process required conscious attempts to withhold selected arbitrary thoughts from becoming speech. However, after a while, all the thoughts began to slow down by themselves, waiting for permission to come out as speech. Gradually, the whole process became automatic with no conscious effort required at all. The person's thoughts learned obedience naturally and did not spill out as speech automatically. With this new self-control, the person finally became their commanding officer[113].

The initial evaluation process gradually disappears and is replaced by an intuitive feeling.

So, it is with deciding what to say. At first, a person actually has to think and evaluate whether the thought that just entered his mind and is waiting to be spoken is *Lashon Hara* or *Rechilus*. After a while however, this evaluation process gradually disappears and is replaced by an intuitive feeling. If the thoughts contain *Lashon Hara* or *Rechilus*, an intuitive feeling of discomfort arises with these thoughts and the person senses a feeling of possible danger if he says them. It is almost as if he develops a sense of smell to the odor of *Lashon Hara* and *Rechilus*. This intuition, this feeling, this sense of danger now becomes his guide. He no longer has to intellectually identify *Lashon Hara* because he can now sense it directly through his intuition. From then on, his conversation is smooth and flowing, intuitively sensing and then stopping any thoughts that may contain prohibitive speech.

Animals have a similar mechanism. They do not think if they are in danger, they instinctively sense it. A person's effort at controlling his speech can eventually achieve this same effortless level. All he has to do is begin. It is for this reason that we have no excuse in front of Hashem concerning our ability to control our Lashon Hara. If we say that it was simply too difficult, His answer will be, "Yes, this is only true in the beginning, but I have given you the possibility to develop it into an intuitive sense and therefore, why didn't you even try?"

The best motive for Shmiras Halashon: Is It Worth It?

What should your ultimate and final motive be to guard your tongue? If you are told that it is a sin in the Torah, you may respond by saying that just as you unfortunately transgress other Mitzvos, so you may transgress this one as well. If you are told that because of *Lashon Hara* the *Moshiach* cannot come, you may respond that you are not sure of the benefits his arrival will bring anyway. But if you are told that by speaking *Lashon Hara* you become your own worst enemy, that you can create powerful accusers in heaven that can wreck your *mazal* and bring you great suffering, you will suddenly stop and reconsider this sin since everyone has a self-protective instinct. It would be best, of course, if you could be motivated to stop this sin simply because Hashem dislikes it but finally, if your only incentive to stop *Lashon Hara* is to prevent your own self-destruction, then this motive would also be quite beneficial.

In many ways deciding to stop speaking *Lashon Hara* is like making a business decision. Every businessman wants to maximize his profits and minimize his losses. His bottom line for every business decision: "Is it worth it"? "Will taking this action lead to greater profit or greater loss?" So, it should be with Lashon Hara. Speaking *Lashon Hara* may bring you some pleasure, increased ego, social approval and even some personal benefit, but is it worth it? Is it worth the losses and suffering that will surely come at a later date because of the accusing angels that you have created in the process? Clearly as a business decision, it is not! Keep this in mind[114].

DAY 19

Chapter Nine

THE PROHIBITION OF LISTENING TO (SHMI'AH) AND BELIEVING IN (KABALA) *LASHON HARA* & *RECHILUS*

The prohibition of listening and believing.

The Torah prohibits the revelation of information that can create damage (Lashon Hara) or animosity (*Rechilus*). Both of these prohibitions relate to the speaker or the revealer of the information. The Torah also prohibits for one to listen to *Lashon Hara* and *Rechilus* or to believe what he hears as being absolutely true[115]. If he is told slanderous information about someone (Lashon Hara), he cannot believe it. If he is told information about what someone said about him or about what someone did to him, which could make him angry (*Rechilus*), he cannot believe it. Rather, he must remain highly skeptical of this revelation and possess serious doubts about its validity. This prohibition is called the prohibition of "kabala" or believing. Since he cannot believe, he should, with all effort, prevent himself from even listening to such conversations in the first place.

The reason for this prohibition: lack of credibility.

Why should believing *Lashon Hara* or *Rechilus* be prohibited? We can understand that slandering someone else or inciting hostility is wrong but if what we hear sounds true, why can't we believe it? What should we do, surgically remove the information from our brains! Shall we deny a revelation that seems to be true and make believe that it is not?

The answer is that you can never really believe *Lashon Hara* and *Rechilus* that is told to you, no matter who told it or under what conditions, unless you investigate it thoroughly yourself[116]. Simply put, the Torah claims that all such remarks lack credibility unless proven otherwise. If you wish to believe any statements besides damaging ones, you can, but regarding statements that can hurt someone or create hostility, you cannot[117]. You no longer have that option. But why should these remarks always lack real credibility? The answer is that it is possible to create false impressions even from statements that on the surface appear to be true. How is this possible?

It is possible to lie even while telling the truth?

It is a well-known fact that when a witness is called in to testify in the secular courts, he is forced to take an oath that he will tell the truth. The oath that is administered is not a simple one. It goes as follows. "Do you, the witness, swear to tell the truth, the whole truth and nothing but the truth?" You will notice that the oath is divided into three parts. Why is this so? It is because the secular courts understand that you can deceive even while telling the truth. The three parts of the oath are designed to prevent this. Let us explain this.

The possibility of lying.

1} "Do you swear to tell the truth?"- Since every person may have a reason to lie, he is asked to swear that he is not lying[118]. He may be lying to get revenge on the defendant. He may be lying to benefit himself in some way if the defendant is convicted. This part of the oath protects against this possibility, the possibility of lying.

The possibility of omission.

2} "Do you swear to tell the whole truth?"- Sometimes a person may tell selected truths and conveniently leave out other facts, which if stated, would create a different impression than that of the original, selected statements[119].

For example:

Little Malky comes to her mother crying that her brother, Sruly kicked her in the knee. The mother goes to Sruly and demands to know if this is true. Sruly responds that it is true but adds that Malky conveniently left out the fact that first she came to him and banged him in the head with a pot.

Was Malky lying? No, but she was not telling the whole truth either and by omitting certain facts, the truth of the event was distorted. This part of the oath protects against this possibility, the possibility of omission.

The possibility of unwarranted and doubtful additions.

3} "Do you swear to tell nothing but the truth?"- Sometimes a person tells the truth but in order to make the story more cohesive, credible or exciting he will embellish it with his own "facts" that he assumes to be true. These additions, however, can actually distort the truth. This part of the oath protects against this scenario, that is, the possibility of unwarranted and doubtful additions.

We see from the above that a person can distort the truth even when he is not lying. This can be done by strategically leaving information out (omissions) or by adding in extras that don't belong there (commissions). There is yet one more way where distortions can occur. This includes:

The possibility of interpreting events negatively.

4} Interpretations - The conversations of most people are not based on facts but rather on their particular perceptions and interpretations of events. When you listen to and believe in a person's remarks, you are actually only accepting his or her particular perceptions and interpretations and not the real and established facts. These interpretations may be only half- true. There may be alternative interpretations that may be much more accurate and truer. They therefore lack true credibility and to believe in them is identical to believing in something that may not be completely true.

Hearing one side of the story

A special case of this type of distortion is when you listen to and believe in only one side of the story. All disputes and disagreements between people are rooted in the ways that each one sees things. Rarely is one view totally correct and the other totally false. There is almost always some truth to both. When someone tells you about someone's negative behavior towards him, it is only his opinion of that person's behavior. There is always another side to the story, that of the other person. To believe one side without knowing the other side is to risk believing only a partial truth. The other side must also be known in order to obtain the whole truth of a conflict[120].

Summary

It is now clear why believing *Lashon Hara* or *Rechilus* is prohibited. Whenever you hear such a statement it may lack credibility because,

1) The person may be lying.
2) He may have omitted important details that could change the impression.
3) He may have added assumed details that distort the truth.
4) He may be interpreting the event in such a way as to be negative.
5) It may be only one side of the story.

Two circumstances when one is permitted to believe Lashon Hara.

Only if you are willing to investigate the events behind the remarks can you know the truth of them. Otherwise, they must remain in doubt. There are two circumstances, however, when you can believe the *Lashon Hara* you hear from a speaker without any investigation (we are assuming that you have permission to listen in the first place).

1) The first is where the speaker is talking *Lashon Hara* only about himself and does not include anyone else[121].

2) The second is where you have also experienced personally, the identical situation being described with the person being talked about and you can therefore verify what the speaker is saying based on your own observations[122].

In all other cases, believing is prohibited without an investigation[123].

DAY 20

Chapter Ten

HOW TO STOP LISTENING TO AND BELIEVING IN *LASHON HARA & RECHILUS*

Techniques to prevent listening.

How does a person protect himself from listening to and believing in the *Lashon Hara* and *Rechilus* that he has heard? There are several useful techniques that everyone should utilize.

Protecting yourself from listening:
- ❖ Avoid people known to continuously speak Lashon Hara[124].
- ❖ Do not join a conversation where *Lashon Hara* is being spoken[125].
- ❖ If you are in a conversation and are suddenly confronted with Lashon Hara, try to change the subject immediately[126].
- ❖ If you cannot, gently remind the speaker that you try to be careful about hearing Lashon Hara[127].
- ❖ If that does not help, try to leave the conversation[128].

If you cannot leave, then:
- ❖ Try not to listen, if possible[129].

- ❖ Make sure not to believe what you are hearing (the main prohibition) [130].
- ❖ Never show any sign of consent or agreement[131].
- ❖ If possible, disagree with the speaker by defending the person being talked about (How does he know? Can there be another interpretation or explanation etc) [132].

Techniques to prevent believing.

Protecting yourself from believing. As soon as you hear *Lashon Hara* (about someone else) or *Rechilus* (as it affects you), question its validity[133]. Examine the information to attempt to invalidate it with the following questions:
- ❖ How does the speaker know this to be true? Did he see it personally, or hear it from someone else and if so, was the third party reliable?
- ❖ Is the speaker lying, leaving something out, or exaggerating?
- ❖ Is it the speaker's interpretation only? How much is actual fact? Is it simply an opinion? Can we give the person spoken about the benefit of the doubt? Maybe the person spoken about meant well? Maybe he had good reasons? Maybe he could not help himself? Maybe there is another explanation or another side of the story?

Giving other people the benefit of the doubt: a safeguard to believing.

Probably, the most important protection device against listening to and believing in *Lashon Hara* and *Rechilus* relates to our attitude about people. Unfortunately, most of us believe that people in general do not have good natures. They can be selfish, arrogant, and greedy. Because of this belief, when we see or hear that people have acted in a certain way that we don't understand, we assume the worst. We interpret their behaviors in a negative way. We rarely, if ever, give them the benefit of the doubt. We are always willing to believe the *Lashon Hara* that we hear since it confirms our deepest feelings about people, that most people aren't really very nice or trustworthy. It is also because of this belief that we allow ourselves to speak *Lashon Hara* about people we don't really understand.

"With righteousness shall you judge your friend"!

The Torah however opposes this attitude and this belief. From the verse, "With righteousness shall you judge your friend" (Vayikra 19:15), *Chazal* tell us that the Torah obligates us to give fellow Jews the benefit of the doubt[134]. It feels that Jews, in general, have goodness in them and are therefore well intentioned in their actions even when they appear inappropriate. Hashem says, "I know my children well and I tell you that they mean well, want to be good and want to do good. They are therefore always to be given the benefit of the doubt." If we followed the Torah's view, we would, because of our positive attitude, be disinclined to slander people or to believe in the slander that is told to us about them. The best defense against speaking *Lashon Hara* and believing in it is to change our negative beliefs about people to a positive one[135].

Most people speak about their family in a positive way.

It is interesting to note that when speaking about our family, we almost always do so in a positive way. We also become very upset at any slanderous statements said about them. We usually refuse to believe in these statements since we have a positive attitude about our family and always give them the benefit of the doubt[136].

What about other Jews? Are they not our family? In Hashem's eyes they surely are since all Jews are brothers and sisters[137] with Him as their father[138]. If we realized that, we would treat all Jews with the same positive attitude that we have for our real family and always give them the benefit of the doubt. There would be no real difference.

How to give other people the benefit of the doubt.

How do we give people the benefit of the doubt? We give people the benefit of the doubt when we consider all the factors that underlie their behavior, both internal and external. We do so by realizing that all actions follow from certain motives and intentions. Even if these actions appear inappropriate, their underlying intentions may not be. If we judge people only on their overt behaviors, the part that is visible to us, and ignore the truth of their underlying intentions, that is, that they may be good, then we would be judging them wrongly. We would be guilty of "package" perceptions which is the tendency to judge something by the external packaging around it and by the way it appears rather than by looking at the thing itself which is in the package and by what it really is.

People are complex. They have minds and souls, and these must be taken into consideration when judging someone. To fail to do so is to judge incompletely and in many cases, to judge mistakenly. Change your beliefs about other Jews and give them the benefit of the doubt. If you do so, you will have developed a powerful shield against speaking or believing *Lashon Hara* and *Rechilus*.

DAY 21

Chapter Eleven

WHEN *LASHON HARA* AND *RECHILUS* ARE PERMITTED

Until now we have been discussing three prohibitions. It is prohibited:

1. To speak *Lashon Hara* because it is forbidden to damage another Jew (principle of damage).
2. To speak *Rechilus* because it is forbidden to create direct hostility between two Jews (principle of hostility).
3. To listen to or believe in *Lashon Hara* and *Rechilus* because it is forbidden to accept harmful information that may not be true (principle of credibility).

Protection as the only reason for permissive Lashon Hara and Rechilus.

There are certain circumstances, however, where one would be permitted to speak either *Lashon Hara* or *Rechilus*. This occurs where the motive for the speech involves the issue of protection. One is permitted to speak *Lashon Hara* or *Rechilus* if he needs to protect himself or another Jew from possible harm or damage[139]. Protection is the only reason that normally prohibited speech becomes permissible. All other motives, such as curiosity, revenge, profit, etc. can never justify *Lashon Hara* or *Rechilus*[140].

The motive of protection overrides against the damage of Lashon Hara and Rechilus.

The Torah mandates the necessity of protecting another Jew both physically and financially. According to *Chazal* this is seen from the verse, "You shall not stand aside while your fellow's blood is shed."[141] The Torah mandates that a potential Jewish victim be protected from a potential Jewish perpetrator or saved from an actual Jewish perpetrator even if to do so requires that *Lashon Hara* or *Rechilus* be spoken against that perpetrator. This principle can be called "the protection override" because the need to protect overrides the prohibition of causing damage (Lashon Hara) or hostility (*Rechilus*)[142].

The Torah considers the need to protect a Jew by speaking *Lashon Hara* if necessary, as greater than the possibility of doing harm to another Jew who is seen as a potential perpetrator. The Torah considers the need to protect a Jew by speaking *Rechilus* if necessary, as greater than the possibility of creating hostility between that Jew and another who is seen as a potential perpetrator.

Two Examples of the "Protection Override".

Let us give an example where this protection override applies. Shimon wants to go into business with Reuven, but he is not sure that Reuven would make a good business partner. He asks Chaim, who happens to know Reuven, what he thinks about such a partnership. Chaim is unsure of what to say. He thinks Reuven is untrustworthy and would not be a good business partner. But if he tells that to Shimon, he would be speaking *Lashon Hara* about Reuven. On the other hand, if he does not warn Shimon about Reuven, Shimon could be potentially harmed in the future. What should he do?

The protection override tells Chaim that he is allowed to harm Reuven by speaking against him in order to save Shimon from future headaches[143]. The need to protect a Jew, Shimon, overrides the harm that can be done to Reuven since he is considered a potential cause of harm to Shimon.

In another example, if Reuven actually threatened to harm Shimon in remarks made to Chaim, then Chaim would surely be obligated to warn Shimon of this threat even though it would cause Shimon to become enraged at Reuven. His warning Shimon would be permitted even though it is *Rechilus* (causing direct anger) since the Torah gives Chaim a protection-override in this matter[144].

Lashon Hara and Rechilus are permitted only for minimal and necessary damage.

Unfortunately, it is still possible to transgress the sin of *Lashon Hara* and *Rechilus* even where one speaks to them to protect another Jew. This is where one ignores the "principle of minimal damage", a critical condition that governs the protection override. This principle states that if a Jew seeks to protect himself or a third party from another Jew by speaking *Lashon Hara* or *Rechilus*, that he does so only by speaking the precise amount of information that is minimally required for protection, and nothing more.

Thus, the protector is permitted to only minimally damage another Jew, that is, not to damage him beyond that which is required for the protection of himself or a third party. If the protector, however, speaks more *Lashon Hara* than is necessary for the protection or if he exaggerates the *Lashon Hara* then he is no longer saved by the protection override since he has excessively damaged another Jew where it was not necessary for this protection[145].

For example, in the case cited before where Shimon asked Chaim whether Reuven was a trustworthy business partner and was told by him that Reuven was not, it would not be forbidden. But if Chaim also said that Reuven was a person who talked too much, that could be *Lashon Hara* since it went beyond the needed information.

Protection-override only if no other means is available.

Similarly, if one can protect oneself or another Jew by using other means besides *Lashon Hara* or *Rechilus*, the principle of minimal damage enjoins him to do so. If he then speaks *Lashon Hara* or *Rechilus* where he did not have to, then the protection override does not apply, and he transgresses the prohibition of *Lashon Hara* or *Rechilus*[146].

It is for this reason that Miriam, Moshe Rabbeinu's sister, was punished, according to some opinions[147]. She spoke *Lashon Hara* about Moshe to Aharon, their brother, so that Aharon could chastise Moshe for a possible error he was making regarding his own wife. It was unnecessary because she could have spoken directly to Moshe and avoided any possibility of *Lashon Hara* and unnecessary damage. Thus, even though her intentions were good, Hashem punished her.

From this principle, we see clearly that if we are having problems with someone, we need to speak directly to them first and not go to a third party right away. Only, if speaking to them first does not help, can we then consider the possibility of eliciting help from a third party[148].

The key factor in determining permissibility is the balance between the protection override and the condition of minimal damage.

The balance between the protection-override and the condition of minimal damage is what determines where speaking *Lashon Hara* and *Rechilus* becomes permissible. Unfortunately, the factors relating to the permissible circumstances can be quite intricate and therefore require a lengthier discussion. This discussion is beyond the scope of this work and therefore, only the general rules have been presented here.

The Protection Override does not apply to believing Lashon Hara and Rechilus.

When it comes to believing *Lashon Hara* or *Rechilus*, the protection override does not apply[149]. The prohibition to believe still exists. You cannot believe the *Lashon Hara* or *Rechilus* told to you even if the reason it was told to you is for your protection. The information may still lack credibility for all the reasons given before. Even if someone speaks *Lashon Hara* solely to protect someone else, it does not add any credibility to this *Lashon Hara* information. It still may not be true or even if it is true, it may not be the whole truth. In addition, it may just be an opinion or only one side of the story. Truth can only be established through an investigation in Beis Din (rabbinical court) regardless of the motives of the protector[150]. It is, however, permitted to listen to this information and consider the possibility of its truth since you must do so in order to protect yourself. The protection override does allow you to listen and to take precautions, but it does not allow you to believe the information that you hear without conducting your own investigation[149].

DAY 22

Chapter Twelve

SUMMARY OF THE LAWS

1. *Lashon Hara*

A. **Definition.** The revelation of information that a person can anticipate will possibly lead to hurting or damaging the well-being of another Jew in any sense, physically, emotionally, financially, socially, or spiritually.
B. **Reason for Prohibition:** The possibility of damage.
C. **Criteria:** *Lashon Hara* is spoken if the revelation
   a. can cause general damage, (or)
   b. can the listener to lose respect, even minimally, for the third party, (or)
   c. can cause the third-party embarrassment if he knew about it.
D. **Permissibility:** Can be spoken if there is a legitimate need to protect oneself or a third party where no other alternative is possible. Can only cause the absolute least amount of damage possible in order to protect and no more[151].

2. *Rechilus*

A. **Definition.** The revelation of information that can be anticipated to directly create hostility between two Jews.
B. **Reason for Prohibition:** Creating hostility, making enemies.
C. **Criteria:** *Rechilus* is spoken if the revelation could cause a Jew to suddenly become resentful or angry at another Jew because of a perceived direct threat coming from that Jew.
D. **Permissibility:** Can be spoken if there is a legitimate need to protect oneself or a third party against present or future damages and where there is no other alternative. Can cause only the minimal hostility necessary to protect and no more.

3. Listening (*Shmi'ah*) and Believing (*Kabalah*)

A. **Definition.** Listening to or believing in information revealed to you without doing a thorough investigation, that can cause you to lose respect for another Jew (Lashon Hara) or to become angry at him because of a perceived direct threat coming from him (*Rechilus*).
B. **Reason for Prohibition:** The problem of credibility.

C. **Criteria:** This prohibition occurs when you allow yourself to listen to the *Lashon Hara* and *Rechilus* that you know is going to be said or you believe and accept this revelation after it was already said without a thorough investigation. You know you believed this if you begin to lose respect for the third party that was spoken about (Lashon Hara) or you begin to feel angry or betrayed by that third party (*Rechilus*).

D. **Permissibility:** It is permitted to listen to any *Lashon Hara* or *Rechilus* told to you if you know in advance that it is for your or a third party's protection from present or future damage (the speaker needs to tell you of this need or you have to ask about it in advance before he speaks) It is always forbidden to believe the information you hear without a thorough investigation even where protection is necessary. You can listen to it and take precautions but not believe it. The need to protect does not give a statement automatic credibility. Only an investigation into the facts can do that.

DAY 23

Chapter Thirteen

HOW TO REPENT FOR THE SIN OF *LASHON HARA* AND *RECHILUS.*

Undoing the damage caused.

When a person speaks *Lashon Hara* or *Rechilus*, how does he repent for his sin? If the person can remember the incidents where he spoke sinfully, that is, if he remembers whom he spoke to and what he spoke about, then the first thing he should do is to try to undo the damage that he caused. He should go back to the listener and attempt to reverse the *Lashon Hara* and *Rechilus* by convincing this person that he made a mistake[152]. He should use the techniques described previously in the section entitled, "How to Stop Believing in *Lashon Hara* and *Rechilus*" by applying it to his own Lashon Hara. Hopefully, the listener will erase his loss of respect (Lashon Hara) or his hostility (*Rechilus*) for the third party spoken about. If there was financial damage involved, he should see to it that he compensates him for his loss[153].

Working on Shmiras Halashon is the best form of repentance.

Unfortunately, in most cases, people just do not remember their past incidents of sinful speech and so

127

they are unable to correct them. How are they to atone to Hashem for their great sins? What are they to do? First, one should fully regret his speaking Lashon Hara and verbally express his remorse on committing this sin (חרטה על העבר וידוי דברים)[154]. The single most important action that a person can take to convince Hashem that he truly regrets his past *Lashon Hara* and that he sincerely repents is to commit himself to make every effort to prevent himself from speaking *Lashon Hara* and *Rechilus* in the future (קבלה על העתיד)[155]. He should concentrate on those techniques previously described. This is especially true of making time every day to learn the laws of *Shmiras Halashon*. If he makes such a sincere effort, Hashem will surely have mercy on him and assist him in achieving a full atonement even for those past transgressions that he can't remember. There are, however, certain additional, highly effective actions that a person can take to atone for the past sins of *Lashon Hara* and *Rechilus*. These include:

Arranging a public Shiur on the laws of Shmiras Halashon.

1) To arrange for or support a public shiur on the laws of *Lashon Hara* for his community or congregation. This puts a person in the category of "benefitting the public "thereby creating for himself a very powerful spiritual merit in his favor that can be used to atone for past Lashon Hara[156].

Participating in a "Machsom Le'fi" group.

2) To arrange for or participate in a "Machsom Le'fi" group. This is a group whose members agree not to speak at all during certain prearranged hours of the day, each member being assigned a different time. This generates powerful spiritual merit for the members of the group and atones for any past Lashon Hara[157].

Forgiving people who speak Lashon Hara about yourself.

3) To state every day in his prayers that he forgives the people who speak *Lashon Hara* and *Rechilus* about him. This action of daily forgiveness awakens great spiritual forces that empower the principle of Mercy to apply towards him[158].

The spiritual effects of repentance for Lashon Hara and Rechilus.

When a person acts to atone for his past sins of *Lashon Hara* and *Rechilus*, powerful spiritual events take place. These events reverse the spiritual damage that he absorbed because of his past Lashon Hara. Let us explain. When a person commits a sin, he creates an accusing angel but without a mouth to accuse him. When he speaks Lashon Hara, this angel suddenly forms a mouth and can therefore begin the actual process of accusation against him in the heavenly court of Justice. When he atones for his past Lashon Hara, however, the mouth that was formed on his accusing angel is suddenly ripped off, rendering this angel speechless once again. The angel can no longer accuse him before the court of Justice in any future related matter.

This is the power of repentance. It restores a person's safety from the eyes of Justice and transfers him to the eyes of Mercy. Even if a person indulges in *Lashon Hara* and arouses great spiritual forces against him, he can still annihilate these forces and restore his safety from them. His *mazal* begins to improve[159]. Repentance for *Lashon Hara* and *Rechilus* should be an absolute priority if a person values his life and wellbeing.

DAY 24

Chapter Fourteen

THE TRUTH OF JEWISH SUFFERING

Shmiras Halashon insures the harmony and survival of the Jewish people even in the face of their transgressions.

The information contained in this booklet is an eye-opener. We finally understand some of the major causes of Jewish suffering and tragedies. The Jewish people can be compared to a person with two legs. Both legs must be working in order to walk and move forward. The first leg is the observance of the Torah and its commandments. This leg is the engine of eternity guaranteeing our place in the world-to-come. It is also the mechanism that grants us peace and opportunity in our physical existence. If this leg is broken, we betray our existence and lose our essential birthright. In addition, we jeopardize the tranquility in our physical lives.

The second leg is the presence of unity and peace and the absence of *Lashon Hara* and *Rechilus* amongst the Jewish people. This leg has the power to act as a crutch, when the first leg, the observance of mitzvos, is weak and we accumulate many sins. It is this second leg acting as a shield that continues to allow us to remain healthy and maintain peace of mind even when the first leg is damaged. It minimizes the suffering that we should experience in our physical existence because of our sins[160]. If this leg is broken, however, we lose our shield and then many troubles befall us according to our sins.

We have forgotten this profound truth.

For the last two thousand years since the destruction of the second Bais Hamikdash, we have given priority to the first leg and ignored the health of the second one. When the first leg became weak and our sins accumulated, the second leg was nowhere to be found. We have forgotten the warning of our *Chazal* about controlling *Lashon Hara* and unwarranted hatred and conflict. We have ignored their warning that the Jewish people cannot afford to be weak in both legs at the same time. The results have been a disaster.

Even in our own time, near the end of history, we remain blind. We see tragedies all around us, but we still ignore the importance of the second leg. This blindness must stop once and for all! We must restore the person (the Jewish people) and make him whole. We must give him back his second leg. Anything less than this is sheer folly.

The restoration of the second leg, guarding one's tongue (Shmiras Halashon) and maintaining brotherhood, must become a Jewish national obsession. We must teach these laws to our children at the earliest possibility. To deny them this information is to condemn them to needless suffering and tragedies. There is no greater way to demonstrate our love for them than to give them this great protective shield of the second leg[161].

DAY 25

Chapter Fifteen

THE ULTIMATE CHALLENGE FOR EVERY JEWISH COMMUNITY

Hashem's search for the Lashon Hara-free community.

Hashem created the world through the attribute of Justice. This means that humans, especially Jews, must create their own eternal destiny through their own efforts. To evaluate their performance, an accusing angel, the Satan, is assigned the task of overseeing this process. When Jewish communities are rife with sins and if, in addition, they contain much conflict, *Lashon Hara* and *Rechilus*, then the Satan continuously reminds Hashem of this situation in his capacity as the angel of Justice. He implores Hashem through the principle of Justice to abandon His Jewish children because of their evil ways saying, "If they rebel against you, their father, and your commandments, it is one thing, but why must they be so evil to themselves, to their own brothers and sisters? These children who have so much hate amongst themselves surely do not deserve a father such as you!"

The Satan is entitled to say these things because of his spiritual assignment. Nevertheless, Hashem, the father, is sorely distressed (so to speak) by these accusations since they are absolutely true. Like any father who loves his children dearly, He does not want to hear of the degradation of His children, no matter what the truth[162].

In response to these terrible accusations, Hashem continuously scans the earth to find at least one Jewish community that is an exception to this situation, where conflicts and *Lashon Hara* barely exist and where brotherly love is the norm. Unfortunately, such a community is yet to be found. If it were found, Hashem, as the father, could reject the universal quality of the Satan's accusations and respond to him by saying, "Look at my children in such and such a place and see how they love and respect each other. See how careful they are with their words so as not to harm each other. For such a community and its merit, I will spare all the other communities and I will never abandon them!"[163]. The power of such a Lashon Hara-free community is so great that even were there only one of them, they could awaken the merits to spare all the others.

The necessary action to create the Lashon Hara-free community.

How would such *a Lashon Hara*-free community be established? Firstly, the community would see to it that every adult member amongst them would have a thorough knowledge of the laws of *Lashon Hara* and

Rechilus. In addition, they would teach this knowledge to all their children starting at an early age. Their educational institutions would continuously focus on this awareness and give it a top priority.

Secondly, their leaders would continuously encourage all communal members never to forget the importance of *Shmiras Halashon* and the absolute necessity for unity and brotherhood. On every possible occasion they would remind the community of the dangers inherent in becoming negligent in this regard.

Thirdly, the leaders would institute that at certain times and during certain hours, the community would participate in a *taanis dibbur* or speech-fast where people would refrain from speaking at all[164]. This would ensure that the sins of any *Lashon Hara* that might have been spoken would be periodically erased and hold no power in Heaven at all.

This most fortunate community would lead the Jewish people to their redemption.

Can such a Jewish community be established? The answer is absolutely yes! Who will be the first? One thing is for certain. This most fortunate community would lead the Jewish people to their redemption[165]. Why not make it yours? Do everything possible to see that this happens. May Hashem grant you much success in this endeavor.

DAY 26

PART THREE

Chapter Sixteen

"OUR FATHER, OUR KING" - !אבינו מלכנו

Hashem is a Father when He is merciful, and He is a King when He is just.

There is a well-known *tefillah* which we say at certain times of the year that starts with the sentence, "Our Father, our King, ("אָבִינוּ מַלְכֵּינוּ") we have sinned before you."[166] In this prayer, we, the Jewish people, refer to Hashem, both as our Father and as our King. What is the meaning of these two titles, Father and King? How are they different?

The title "our Father" refers to Him when He acts through the principle of Mercy. When He is compassionate and loving, we say that He is acting as our Father. The title "our King", on the other hand, refers to Him when He acts through the principle of Justice. When He is righteous and judges us, we say that He is acting as our King[167].

Hashem, as our Father, loves us dearly and wants only the best for us.

If we further examine the difference between Hashem as our Father and Hashem as our King, we see that there are even more distinctions. Hashem, as our Father, loves us dearly and wants only the best for us. Moreover, as our Father, He considers us as His family, His sons and daughters. As a family, He expects us to act as brothers and sisters toward one another. He wants us to demonstrate respect, love and caring amongst ourselves. He wants to see acts of kindness and a deep concern for each other's safety and welfare[168].

Hashem, as our King, expects us to act as law-abiding citizens showing mutual respect.

Hashem, as our King, on the other hand, mainly respects us and wants to see us prosper. Moreover, as our King, Hashem considers us as the subjects of His kingdom. As subjects in His kingdom, He expects us to act as law-abiding citizens. He wants us to show mutual respect for the rights and property of one another even if on a personal level, we regard each other as strangers.

Clearly then, Hashem as a Father and Hashem as a King relate to the Jewish people differently. The former is focused on love and mercy. The latter is focused on truth and justice. The former sees the Jewish people as a family and requires them to love as well as to respect each other. The latter sees them as subjects and requires them mainly to respect each other even if on a personal level they are strangers.

We always request that Hashem be our Father first and then our King.

Hashem is always both our Father and our King since He treats us with both mercy and justice. We see this clearly in the prayer mentioned before ("Avinu, Malkeinu"). As such, we are always both His family and His subjects. However, Hashem does not always interact with us as a Father and as a King equally, at the same time. There are times when His attribute of Mercy is dominant, and He is much more like our Father (*kvi'yachol*). There are other times when his attribute of Justice is more dominant, and He is much more like our King and Judge.

This predominance of one attribute over the other can also be clearly seen in the prayer mentioned above particularly in its chosen sequence of Father and King. In that prayer, we first say, "our Father" and only after that do we say "our King". By saying it in this order, we are indicating our preference, and are requesting that Hashem's *Father* aspect, dominate. We are asking that He prioritize His mercy over His justice. If our prayers are accepted, we will be showered with compassion. However, if our prayers are not accepted, then it means that in Heaven, Hashem's *King* aspect dominates over

His *Father* aspect, and He is prioritizing His justice over His mercy. In such a case, we will be showered with the serious consequences of justice. It is as if Hashem disagrees with our version and transmits to us His version of the prayer which is "Our King, Our Father" and not "Our Father, Our King".

DAY 27

The Jewish people can control the dominance of mercy over justice by the way they treat each other.

Can we, the Jewish people, actually control the sequence of Father and King as it appears in Hashem's version of the prayer so that we can control which aspect dominates? In other words, can we influence Hashem (*kviyachol*) to be a Father first and a King second? The answer is yes! We do this by taking advantage of the principle of "measure for measure".

The Talmud teaches us that our actions before Hashem influence His actions towards us[169]. If we Jews act towards each other as a family by demonstrating love and caring, we influence Hashem's aspect of Father to dominate since we are meeting His expectations as a Father. Mercy then abounds[170]. On the other hand, if we act as strangers towards each other, then we influence Hashem's aspect of King to dominate since we are only meeting His expectations as a King. Justice then reigns. It is in our hands, measure for measure. We control the sequence of Father and King in His version of the prayer and choose which aspect will dominate by the way we treat and interact with each other, as family or as strangers.

When Jews ignore each other's dangers, then Hashem acts as a King treating them with strict justice.

Hashem always desires to be primarily our Father and treat us with great mercy. As such, He considers us primarily as His family. It is possible, however, to corrupt our behavior so that this normal status of family is altered and suddenly, we are reduced to the lower status of subjects in His kingdom. How corrupt must our behavior be towards each other in order to finally lose the title of family completely and assume the title of stranger and subject? In other words, how inferior must our interactions be with each other before Hashem finally considers us as a group of strangers where He treats us as a King, with justice being the dominant attribute?

The answer is surprising. In Hashem's view, so to speak, even when we are in conflict with each other and even when we indulge in Lashon Hara, we are still considered a family since this type of behavior can be seen in many families[171]. However, if we see that our brothers and sisters from a particular segment of the Jewish people are in real danger and we callously disregard this by conducting our lives as if nothing has happened, then we are no longer acting as a family. This is because even though a true family can fight amongst themselves, nevertheless, they would never ignore each other's danger.

By refraining from praying for endangered brothers we lose all claim to the title of family.

Furthermore, if we become so indifferent that we even refrain from at least crying out and praying to Hashem to save our endangered brothers and sisters, then at that point, because of our gross insensitivity, we lose all claim to the title of family as far as Heaven is concerned. From then on, Hashem considers us, the Jewish people, as a nation of strangers and treats us as mere subjects of His Kingdom. His King aspect dominates, and He dispenses strict justice.

If, on the other hand, we recognize our fellow Jews' danger and we at least pray for them in their hour of distress, then Hashem still sees us as a family and treats us with mercy and love despite the fact that we indulge in *Lashon Hara* and controversy and we lack communal unity. The reason for this is that by minimally praying for each other, we fulfill the commandment, "You shall not stand aside while your fellow's blood is shed",[172] and because of this we are still considered a family.

The matter now becomes clear. If we ignore this commandment by being a passive witness to each other's danger and possible destruction where even prayer is excluded, then it is through this that we completely destroy our brotherhood and family status. It is this circumstance that makes us suddenly vulnerable to strict justice for our transgressions and creates the possibility of great tragedies befalling us. The presence of controversy, *Lashon Hara,* and elitism amongst us does not, by itself, destroy the Jewish people as a family. Callous insensitivity and disregard for each other's danger does and especially where even prayer has been abandoned.

DAY 28

Chapter Seventeen

THE MOST POWERFUL PRAYER OF ALL

A powerful prayer is one that moves Hashem, kviyachol, to become primarily a Father, (merciful).

We clearly see that Hashem relates to us as both a Father (mercy) and a King (justice). We also now see that we, the Jewish people, can control which of these two aspects will dominate by the way we interact with each other, that is, as a family or as strangers. This new knowledge gives us great spiritual power, that is, the power to control our destiny and the events that overtake us.

The fact that Hashem relates to us in two different aspects also has an important bearing on the effectiveness of our prayers to him. By understanding the connection between His two aspects and our prayers, we can construct prayers that suddenly become very powerful spiritual weapons. We can create the ultimate power prayer.

What precisely is the power prayer? All prayers are measured in terms of two characteristics. The first is a prayer's effectiveness and the second is a prayer's power. A prayer's effectiveness is its ability to make itself heard and be accepted before Hashem. A prayer's power is its ability, due to its internal content, to move Hashem (so to speak) towards His Father aspect and away from His King aspect. Clearly, the greater a prayer's power and ability to evoke Hashem's Father aspect, the greater becomes its effectiveness in being heard and accepted. A prayer that can successfully do this is called a power prayer. If this prayer is said conscientiously and with sincerity, it can become an extraordinary powerful weapon in the hands of an individual Jew or a complete community[173].

If we follow this idea to its conclusion, we become aware of the existence of the most powerful prayer of all. What is the most powerful prayer of all? It is the prayer that has the power to break the walls of Heaven and forcefully present itself in front of the throne of Hashem Himself with no counter-force capable of stopping it. It is a prayer that has no equal in moving Hashem (so to speak) to become a Father almost exclusively thereby opening the wellsprings of mercy. Let us see what such a prayer contains.

There are three levels of a prayer's power.

There are fundamentally, three levels of prayer that can be measured in terms of their effectiveness and power.

A Jew who is praying only for himself.

Level 1: A Jew in distress prays for himself so that Hashem will extricate him from that distress. The power of this prayer is weak and especially if the person possesses no special merits. The reason for this is that since he is in distress, he has obviously been convicted and sentenced by the heavenly court of Justice for certain misdeeds. His status is, therefore, that of convicted defendant throwing himself at the mercy of the court. His prayer is weak since he faces Hashem, the King and judge, where justice dominates.

A Jew who prays not only for himself but also for another Jew who shares his distress.

Level 2: A Jew in distress prays for himself and also for another Jew who is facing a similar distress so that Hashem will extricate them both from that distress. The power of this prayer is much stronger than the one mentioned before (level 1) even if both of them possess no special merit. By praying for another Jew in addition to praying for himself, he is indicating that he cares for that other Jew as a brother and a family member. By declaring this family connection, then measure for measure, Hashem is influenced to become primarily a Father where mercy is the dominant attribute. Hashem then extricates the first Jew who prays from his distress because the Father and mercy aspects now dominate.

The second Jew who is prayed for can also be redeemed because, having been influenced to become primarily a Father, Hashem can now apply mercy to affect him as well. However, since the first Jew who prays is the one who evoked Hashem's Father aspect through his prayers, Hashem answers and redeems him first before he redeems the second Jew[174].

This level of prayer does have a weakness, however. The primary motive for praying for another Jew was that this other Jew shared a similar distress and that as long as he was praying for himself, he might as well include the other Jew as well. It can be argued, however, that were there no need to pray for himself, then he probably would not have prayed for this other Jew at all. This prayer then, with its questionable motives of true brotherhood, loses some of its effectiveness. Nevertheless, it can still be powerful as indeed we find that such a level of prayer was able to redeem the Jews from Egypt.

We see this from the following. In Parshas Va'eira[175], Hashem says of the Jews in bondage, "And I have **also** (וגם אני) heard the cry of distress of the sons of Israel....and I have remembered my covenant." The Chasam Sofer[176] asks the question, "What does Hashem mean when He says, I, also? Who else can be hearing their cries?" He answers that all the Jews in bondage heard each other's cries and saw each other's suffering. Because of this they assisted and prayed for each other.

To this, Hashem says, "I also", that is, I hear their cries in addition to all of you who hear each other's cry and pray for each other. If I, Hashem, become an "also", it means that you, the Jewish people, have become a true family of brothers and sisters who see each other's pain. Measure for measure, I will become primarily a Father where mercy dominates and I will redeem you from slavery.

A Jew who prays for another Jew without sharing his distress.

Level 3: A Jew prays for another Jew who is in distress even though he does not share this distress at all so that Hashem will extricate that Jew from his troubles. This is the most powerful prayer of all and its ability to influence Hashem to become a Father and be merciful has no equal. It shatters every wall in Heaven and forcefully presents itself before Hashem with no counter-force capable of stopping it. It is the ultimate "power prayer".

The only motive for this prayer is pure brotherhood and the love of a fellow Jew.

When a Jew who is not in distress prays for another Jew who is, the only motive for this prayer is pure brotherhood and the love of a fellow Jew. The principle of measure for measure is powerfully activated and Hashem becomes almost a complete and merciful Father both to the first Jew who prays and to the second Jew he is praying for. He is a Father to the first Jew who prays because of his demonstrated brotherhood. This Jew can then benefit from a powerful mercy for his own transgressions. Hashem is a Father to the second Jew in distress because of the inherent argument presented by the first Jew who prays, who indicates by his prayers that, "if I can cry out for my fellow Jew as a brother, how can you, Hashem, ignore him as a father!" The Jew in distress can now benefit from a special mercy directed at him. Such is the power of this prayer that if said by many people, it can potentially redeem almost every Jew in crisis, no matter how negative the circumstances.

DAY 29

Chapter Eighteen

The Obligation To Use The Power Prayer To Redeem Other Jews

The power groups are Jews who have a greater power to pray for other Jews.

There are certain Jewish groups that have a greater power to redeem a selected population of Jews in distress through their prayers than other groups. These groups are considered the ultimate "power groups" to redeem these selected Jewish populations. A power group is a group that has the ability to utter a power prayer. We have seen that this refers to a group that prays for other Jews in need or distress where they themselves do not have that need or share that distress (level 3). If that group did have that need or shared that distress, then their prayers would be less effective, and they would not be a true power group (level 2).

Two groups of Jews who are currently in danger are those who are in the process of assimilating and those who live in Eretz Yisroel.

There are two groups of Jews in the world who are currently in great danger. It is very important to know who these endangered groups are and who the power groups are that can possibly redeem them through their prayers. The first group is that of the millions of Jews worldwide who are currently in the process of losing their Jewish identity through assimilation and intermarriage. It is estimated that in twenty years over five million Jews will be lost, in the United States alone. If this process is not stopped, they will be lost to the Jewish people forever. The Jewish power group that could redeem this group in danger through their prayers would be composed of all Jews, wherever they are, who are Torah observant and who consequently do not share the endangered Jews' crisis of assimilation. Their prayers on behalf of their endangered brothers and sisters could successfully influence Hashem to become merciful as a Father and stay the process of assimilation. The second group is that of the millions of Jews in the land of Israel who are currently being threatened by millions of Arab enemies waiting to destroy them. If these enemies are even partially successful, the results would be catastrophic. The Jewish power group that could redeem this group in danger through their prayers would be composed of all those Jews who live outside of the land of Israel and who consequently are not physically endangered. Their prayers on behalf of their endangered brothers and sisters could successfully influence Hashem to become merciful as a Father and remove the threatening circumstances facing them.

Jews are obligated to pray for each other's welfare.

There is a compelling obligation for all Jews and especially for all those that can be considered power groups, to help save their endangered brothers and sisters through prayer. This is true for two reasons: Firstly, there is a specific commandment in the Torah that obligates every Jew to exert all possible efforts in this direction. "You shall not stand aside while your fellow's blood is shed" (Vayikra 19:16). "Your fellow's blood" would include all physical and spiritual dangers and "standing aside" would include not even praying for them. Secondly, Jews need to do this for their own salvation and for their own protection from their transgressions. When Jews callously disregard each other's danger, they break the bonds that unite them as a family unit. Hashem considers this callous disregard as a terminal sign that the Jews have ceased to be a family and have instead become a group of strangers since true family members would never act that way. Thereupon, Hashem withdraws His Father and mercy aspect and instead shows Himself as a King and Judge where justice dominates. The Jews will then experience strict justice that would be seen in the many troubles that would befall them because of their transgressions. This reason, therefore, obligates all Jews to minimally pray for their endangered brothers because if they do not, they risk being dominated by Hashem's king-aspect of strict justice from then on and rarely will they see the merciful hand of their father.

Source that one is obligated to pray for the welfare of other Jews.

The obligation to pray for the welfare of other Jews has already been taught by one of our greatest sages[177]. Rabbeinu Yonah in his *Sefer HaYir'ah*[178], states the following:

"If you hear the trouble of distant Jews*[179]*, groan and pray for them. One should pray every day to the Holy One, blessed be He, according to his customary language, for the Jewish people, that is, for their rehabilitation from all illness, for their redemption from amongst the gentile nations, for their salvation from all ill-fortunes, for the release of all their imprisoned, for the spiritual enlightenment of those who are captured in the darkness of the gentiles, for their approach to true repentance and that the Holy One, blessed be He, should accept them before Him."

Ignoring another Jew's danger causes Hashem to become (so to speak) enraged and brings down severe Justice.

This compelling obligation should not be taken lightly. This would be a catastrophic mistake. Indeed, if you should ask, bottom line, what is the single greatest sin that the Jews have transgressed throughout their history that is more responsible than any other for causing their horrific disasters, it would surely be their failure to live up to this obligation of not standing by their brothers' blood with at least an outcry to Hashem to save them. There is nothing that so enrages Hashem (so to speak) more and provokes His immediate justice to descend upon the Jews than His watching them sit by and do nothing while a segment of their family, other Jews, face terrible danger. If you doubt this, then consider the following scenario.

You are a parent of two adult sons. One is swimming in a lake near the shore while the other is relaxing on the shore. Nearby sits a lifeguard. Suddenly, the son swimming in the lake develops a leg cramp and begins to drown. The other son on the shore sees this and strangely, he continues to relax. Moreover, he is so indifferent to his brother's terrible predicament that he even fails to alert the lifeguard about the situation. You, the parent, have observed this entire scenario. How would you feel? The answer is obvious. You would become greatly outraged at your son relaxing on the shore. If he claimed that there was nothing he could do since he cannot swim, you would accuse him of not even bothering to call the lifeguard, the least action he could have taken. If Hashem forbid, your other son had actually drowned, you would probably either disown this one and never speak with him again or severely punish him because of his callous disregard for his brother's life.

Hashem's reaction, should He see such a similar scenario amongst His children, the Jewish people, would be similar to yours, the parent. If He sees that Jews are callously indifferent to the dangers, spiritual and physical, facing their fellow Jews, He becomes enraged (so to speak). Should these indifferent Jews then defend themselves by claiming that there was nothing that they could do, Hashem would then respond as the parent would and say, "Why didn't you at least call over the lifeguard and plead with him to save your brother's life?" Hashem, of course, would be referring to himself as the ultimate lifeguard. Even though He already knows of the dangers these Jews are facing since He is causing them for His own inscrutable reasons (therefore He need not be alerted that they are in danger), nevertheless, by calling to Him to save these Jews as a brother, He could then become a lifeguard, that is, be primarily a Father and dispense mercy.

More specifically, Hashem would respond as follows. "Your claim that you were so powerless to save your fellow Jews is not true. I am the G-d of all existence and therefore nothing can happen that is beyond my knowledge, consent, and control. If a segment of the Jewish people is in a crisis and danger, it is because of My will and My decree. I am the cause of that crisis and therefore I can be the cause of its dissolution. You know this to be true. Why then did you not turn to me and plead with me to save your brother Jew by reversing that decree? Why didn't you cry out to me of your pain and agony in witnessing his sorrow and despair? Why didn't you plead with me, as my children, for your brothers' sake and beg me to show the compassion of a father? Your pleas could have been my justification to the Satan, the accuser, that I must turn aside from my role as a King and Judge in the world and instead preside as a Father because by your pleading to me for your brothers, you have acted as a family. If you could do nothing else, you could have done this. Where was your outcry (tz'akah)?"

DAY 30

When one Jew prays for another Jew, he should do so for all endangered Jews without exception.

It is very important that the prayer said for endangered Jews not be selective, that is, that it focuses only on a certain endangered group while conspicuously ignoring another endangered group. In such a case, the prayers could become essentially ineffective even for the group that is being prayed for since the Jews who utter these prayers can be accused of selective brotherhood, that is, favoring certain brothers over others. Hashem the Father would then be sorely disturbed (so to speak) and Hashem the King would emerge as dominant.

This selectivity, unfortunately, is often seen in the prayers of Torah observant Jews who specifically pray only for their own group's welfare (especially as regards the sick and unfortunate) while ignoring the great dangers facing other Jews. This exclusion is most dramatically seen when it comes to the danger facing the non-orthodox Jews (especially in America), which is their potential spiritual annihilation. In doing so, Torah observant Jews fail to realize that by neglecting the dangers facing the non-orthodox in their prayers, they are jeopardizing their prayers' ability to be heard and accepted even for their own group since these prayers lack the ability to awaken Hashem's Father aspect because of their selected brotherhood. Therefore, if Torah observant Jews want their prayers accepted in Heaven for themselves, they must include all other significantly, endangered Jews as well.

A significant reason for this neglect is that, unfortunately, many Torah observant Jews remain amazingly ignorant of their power of prayer for the millions of non-observant Jews who are assimilating and facing spiritual annihilation. They have a mistaken belief that there is nothing that they can do. They do not realize that to a large degree this threat to the non-observant community is really a decree from the heavenly court of Justice and as such is subject to modification by the principle of mercy. They do not realize that it is in their power to awaken this mercy by their prayers since it demonstrates true brotherhood.

One of the most powerful accusations of the Satan against Torah observant Jews is undoubtedly the fact that they have not extended themselves to forcefully cry out for the salvation of the non-observant before Hashem, the Father of all Jews. The Satan constantly declares before Hashem that Torah observant Jews do not really care for their brothers, the non-observant Jews, since they do not demonstrate an outcry of pain and agony at the fact that they are witnessing nothing less than a spiritual holocaust that is about to engulf them. The Satan further asks Hashem as to why, in such a case, should He transcend his judgment and grant mercy for the non-observant. Torah observant Jews also fail to grasp the fact that their minimal outreach efforts towards the non-orthodox to make them Torah observant will never truly succeed as long as they perceive this group of Jews as unworthy of a supreme effort to plead with Hashem on their behalf to save them.

Torah observant Jews must correct this mistake before it is too late. They must vigilantly declare before Hashem that the horror of watching five million Jews disappear from Jewry is unbearable. Hashem awaits their outcry and prayers so that He can turn to the Satan and say, "if my children, the Torah observant Jews, can plead for their less fortunate brothers, the non-observant, how can I, the Father of them all, turn away and ignore their cries!" There is no greater power group to redeem the non-observant from their crisis than Torah observant Jews. They have a great responsibility which they must not ignore. Should they fulfill this obligation, then Hashem's joy would be enormous and the benefit that they would receive would be indescribable.

Chapter Nineteen

The Most Powerful Jewish Community of All

Who is the most powerful Jewish community of all? It is that community whose members are Torah observant Jews focusing on the diligent observance of all the commandments that relate to Hashem and to their fellow Jews. This would be the optimal circumstance. Minimally, however, there is another circumstance that could qualify a community for this title. Even where a Jewish community was lax or negligent in their Torah observance, if they could, through their actions, consistently influence Hashem to exercise His Father and mercy vaspect towards them, they would also be considered very powerful as well. How would they do this? They would do this by demonstrating the two behaviors that most enable Hashem's mercy to dominate. They are,

 A. The steadfast absence of *Lashon Hara* and *Rechilus*

 B. Being constantly alert to the dangers facing Jews everywhere, both spiritual and physical, and never ceasing to implore Hashem through their prayers to be merciful and redemptive to these endangered Jews.

Many tragedies that we have experienced could have been diminished or even prevented.

Had the Jewish people throughout their history demonstrated even only this latter action in the way described, then most of the tragedies that they experienced could have been diminished or even prevented.

The purpose of this booklet is to help empower the Jewish people through these two ways. By discussing the essential laws of *Lashon Hara* and *Rechilus* and by explaining the power and obligation of the redemptive prayers, it is hoped that this will be accomplished.

When will the Jewish people awaken? When will they demonstrate their true power and take charge of their destiny? When will they do what it takes to shower themselves with mercy from Hashem, the Father and not justice from Hashem, the King? When will they confront and weaken their accusing angels so that they experience only the barest of national and personal troubles? The hour is late, and the time is now. Let us all rise to the occasion and give honor and *nachas* to Hashem, the Father and the King. Amen, may it be His will.

Sources & Footnotes

Part One

1. ראה מלכים א, טז ואילך.
2. ראה שמואל ב, א.
3. ירושלמי פאה, פרק א הלכה א. מדרש רבה, דברים ה.
4. מכות כג, ב.
5. עי' נדרים לט, ב; ועי' ירושלמי פאה א, א: השוה הכתוב מצוה קלה שבקלות וכו' למצוה חמורה שבחמורות.
6. עי' בספר "שערי תשובה" לרבנו יונה, שער שלישי, שָׁמְנָה שם כמעט כל מצוות התורה בי' (או י"א) מדרגות, ע"ש.
7. ערכין טו, ב.
8. שמות כ, יב.
9. יומא ט, ב.
10. ראה בהקדמה לספר חפץ חיים.
11. ברייתא ראש השנה יח, ב. וראה בשו"ע או"ח סי' תקמט, א. ובמשנה ברורה שם ס"ק א שהוא מדברי הנביאים (זכריה ח, יט).
12. גמ' ראש השנה (שם).
13. עי' משנה ברורה שם. ומקורו מדברי הרמב"ם בהל' תענית פרק ה, א. ועי' 'חובת השמירה' להח"ח ז"ל פ"ח.
14. ירושלמי יומא א, א. מדרש שוחר טוב קלז, י.
15. חיד"א, דברים אחדים דרוש לא; וראה בארוכה בדרשתו האחרונה של הגאון רבי רפאל האמבורגער ז"ל, בס' זכר צדיק, וז"ל: "הביטו נא וראו בעין הבחינה הנכונה, **כי מיום ברא ה' א'לקים אדם על הארץ עד היום הזה, כל אשר עבר עלינו, חטאת הלשון היתה בעוכרינו... גם כל המאורעות והצרות אשר עברו עלינו זה יותר מאלף ושבע מאות שנה אשר נפזרנו בגולה בארבע כנפות הארץ, סיבת כולן הלא הוא העוון הרע הזה אשר עדיין מרקד בינינו"**. וראה חפץ חיים בהקדמה; מהר"ל נתיבות עולם, נתיב הלשון פ"ט; חיד"א, דברים אחדים דרוש לא; של"ה הק' ווי העמודים עמוד השלום פרק כז, ועוד.
16. ראה חפץ חיים הלכות לה"ר כלל ט, ה: "אם נחנך את הילדים מקטנותם בעניין שמירת הלשון, ממילא יהי' דבר זה נטוע בנפשם מצד ההרגל, והי' נקל להם אח"כ לגדור את עצמם לגמרי במדה הקדושה ההיא, והיו זוכין עבור זה לחיי עולם הבא ולכל טוב בעולם הזה". ובמכתב מהג"ר יהודה זאב סג"ל ז"ל, ראש ישיבת מאנטשעסטער, כתב ע"ז: "דבריו הקדושים אלו (של החח"ח), לא זו בלבד שהם עצה טובה ומועילה, אלא **שהם מגלים האחריות הגדול והנורא המוטל על האבות והמלמדים והמחנכים בני ובנות ישראל, שבידינו להציל מהעבירות החמורים התלויות באי שמירת הלשון**, ומכל הדברים הרעים הבאים בכלל זה, ולזכותם ולרומם אותם למדרגות גדולות. **מה גדול ונורא האחריות, ומה נשיב ליום הדין על שמנענו הטוב מהם, אם לא נשתדל בזה".**
17. עיין כל זה בארוכה בספר 'דרך ה'' לרמח"ל, ח"א פ"ב בתכלית הבריאה. דעת תבונות אות יח. ועי' מסילת ישרים ריש פרק א. ובפתיחה לס' חפץ חיים מ"ש בשם הרמב"ן.

18. דעת תבונות שם, ע"פ הירושלמי ערלה א, ג. וראה בס' מגיד מישרים למרן מהרי"י קארו פ' בראשית.
19. דעת תבונות אות מ, מג-מד, מח בביאור ענין הבחירה. וע"ע בספר 'דרך ה"' (שם).
20. ב'דרך ה"' (ח"א פרק ד, י) כתב: "בכל מעשה [מצוה] מהן שיעשה, יהיה מתקרב על ידו מדרגה מה ממדרגות הקורבה אליו יתברך שמו, ותגיע לו על ידי זה מדרגה מה ממדרגות הארת פניו, כפי הקורבה אליו יתברך שמו, ותתעצם בו מדרגה מן השלימות, שהיא תולדת מדרגת ההארה ההיא, והיפך זה העבירה".
21. דרך ה' (ח"ב פרק ח).
22. ברכות נח, א. וע' ירושלמי ראש השנה א, א. פסיקתא רבתי מא.
23. ראה בארוכה 'דרך ה"' (ח"ב פרק ו).
24. ראה בבא בתרא טז, א: הוא שטן (המקטרג), הוא יצר הרע (המסית ומפתה) הוא מלאך המות (המעניש).
25. חולין ז, ב.
26. ראה מסילת ישרים סוף פרק ד, בביאור מהות התשובה.
27. ראה 'דרך ה"' (ח"ב פ"ו א-ג). וזה ענין 'הקב"ה עומד מכסא דין ויושב על כסא רחמים' המבואר בחז"ל בכמה מקומות. ראה לדוגמא גמ' עבודה זרה ג, ב. מדרש רבה, ויקרא כט.
28. מסילת ישרים, שם.
29. ראה זוהר חדש מג, ב: "אותה שעה גער הקב"ה בסמ' שדיבר לשון הרע על ישראל".
30. מגילה יב, ב ועוד.
31. שמירת הלשון, שער הזכירה פ"ב בארוכה; שמירת הלשון ח"ב פ"ד; אהל יעקב להמגיד מדובנא פרשת מצורע, ועוד.
32. ראה בשמירת הלשון שם: "דידוע הוא דאהבת הקדוש ברוך הוא לעמו ישראל הוא עד מאוד... והוא רואהו שאינו מתנהג כשורה, אף על פי כן הוא מחפה עליו מרוב אהבתו אותו, ואף אם ייסרנו לפעמים, יהי' ברוב חנינה וחמלה...", עיין שם. וראה ב'זכור למרים' (למרן בעל חפץ חיים זצ"ל) פ"ג.
33. ראה ב'זכור למרים' פ"ג מש"כ מרן בעל חפץ חיים זצ"ל, וזה לשונו: "הנה הכתוב אומר (משלי יט, כא): 'רבות מחשבות בלב איש, ועצת ה' היא תקום". ונבאר עצתו של הקב"ה בענין זה. דאיתא במדרש שאמר הקב"ה: "מכל הצרות הבאות עליכם אני יכול להציל אתכם, ומ"שוט לשון תחבא" (איוב ה, כא). וביאור הענין, שהקב"ה, שהוא מקור החסד והרחמים, כדכתיב בקרא, וגם היום חסדיו ורחמיו לא כלו, כדכתיב (איכה ג, כב) חסדי ה' כי לא תמנו, כי לא כלו רחמיו, **רצונו לחפות על כל דבר ולמצוא צד זכות**, אכן בתנאי שלא יעמוד השטן כנגד כסא הכבוד לקטרג. ובעל הלשון הרע, העומד למטה בארץ ומדבר על חביריו רכילות ולשון הרע ומחלוקת וכהאי גוונא, **הוא הוא הנותן לו פה לקטרג**, כמבואר בזוהר הקדוש".
34. מסכת פאה, פרק א הלכה א.
35. ראה מלכים א, טז ואילך.
36. מדרש שוחר טוב, תהלים יב.
37. וגם שאול המלך ושלשת בניו מתו במלחמה - ראה שמואל א, פרק לא.
38. מדרש רבה, דברים ה.
39. פרשת כי תצא, סוף רמז תתקלג.
40. פרשת פקודי רסד, ב.
41. עיין מה שהביא בספר 'רשפי אש' להרה"ק רבי מרדכי מנעשכיז זצ"ל בשם רבינו הבעש"ט הק' זי"ע בביאור הפסוק (שמות כג, א) "לא תשא שמע שוא, אל תשת ידך עם

רשע להיות עד חמס". וביתר ביאור בהקדמת 'לקוטי תורה וש"ס' להרה"ק רבי יצחק אייזיק מזידיטשויב זצ"ל בשם הרה"ק רבי משה מפשעוואורסק זצ"ל. וע' בס' "אש דת" להרה"ק מאוז'רוב זצ"ל פרשת קדושים, ע"ש.

42. בראשית כז, כב.
43. מכילתא, בשלח יד, מדרש תהלים כב.
44. שופטים פרק ז-ח.
45. מלכים ב, פרק יח-יט.
46. תהלים כ, ח-ט.
47. על דיבורי תפילה שאינם עולים למעלה – ראה שמירת הלשון שער הזכירה פרק ז מה שהביא מהזוה"ק בפרשת מצורע. ועל דיבורי תורה – ראה חפץ חיים בהקדמה; 'כבוד שמים' למרן בעל חפץ חיים זצ"ל, פ"א ופ"ו. ומקורו טהור מהזוה"ק בפרשת פקודי. ועיין שבת קיט, ב. שמירת הלשון, שער הזכירה פ"ז.
48. עי' מגילה כח, א.
49. ע' זוה"ק שמות קלא. וראה משנ"ב או"ח קנא, ב. וע' בפתיחה לספר ח"ח עשין ז.
50. ראה משלי יג, יג: 'בז לדבר יחבל לו'. וע' משנת רבי אהרן לחודש אלול.

Part Two

51. רמב"ם הלכות דעות ז, ה: "והמספר דברים שגורמים - אם נשמעו איש מפי איש – להזיק חברו בגופו או בממונו, ואפילו להצר לו או להפחידו, הרי זה לשון הרע". וכתב החח"ח (לשה"ר כלל ה, ו): "על כן קשה מאוד להעתיק בספר כל הענינים שנכשלים בו בענין לשון הרע, רק קח דברי הרמב"ם (הנ"ל) עטרה לראשך, וזכור אותו תמיד".
52. חפץ חיים, הלכות לשה"ר כלל א, ח. ושם סעיף יד. ראה רש"י מלכים א ב, ה בשם התנחומא.
53. חפץ חיים, הלכות לשה"ר כלל א, ח. ובבאר מים חיים (שם) ע"פ רש"י פ' קדושים. וראה משלי ו, יב-יג.
54. ולכן השתמשנו הרבה במלה "גילוי" – כי יסוד האיסור הוא ל ג ל ו ת ע מ י ד ע שיכול לגרום היזק או בושה, ואין נפק"מ אם הגילוי נעשה ע"י דיבור או ע"י הבעת פנים או כתיבה וכדומה, בכל אופן הגילוי אסור.
55. רמב"ם שם הלכה ב. ובח"ח הל' לשה"ר כלל א, א. ובבאמ"ח שם בארוכה.
56. רמב"ם שם.
57. מדרש רבה, במדבר ט.
58. ראה שמירת הלשון, שער התבונה פ"ו. וע"ש מה שהביא מהירושלמי (נדרים פרק ט, הלכה ד) משל נפלא בענין זה.
59. עי' לעיל הערה ??.
60. חפץ חיים, הלכות לשה"ר כלל ג, ד ע"פ הירושלמי, והוא הנקרא 'לשון הרע בצינעא'.
61. חפץ חיים, הלכות לשה"ר כלל ב, יג. וראה בהערה הקודמת.
62. שם כלל ג, ד. ובבאמ"ח שם.
63. שם, הלכה ו.
64. שם כלל ה, ב. וכלל ו, א.
65. שם כלל ב, א.
66. שם כלל ד, א ובבאמ"ח בארוכה.

67. באר מים חיים כלל ד, ס"ק מו. ע"פ הגמ' בנזיר כג,א. וע" בית הלוי פרשת וישלח עה"פ כי נבלה עשה בישראל (בראשית לד, ז).
68. כדין כל ספיקא דאורייתא דאזלינן לחומרא (ביצה ג, ב ועוד).
69. שם, כלל א, ה.
70. שם, כלל ג, ד.
71. שם, כלל ה, ג.
72. באר מים חיים כלל ד, ס"ק לב תנאי ד. וכן בח"ח שם, כלל י, ב (תנאי ה).
73. שם, כלל א, ז.
74. שם, כלל ג, ג.
75. שם, כלל א, ה.
76. שם.
77. שם, כלל א, ו.
78. שם.
79. שם, כלל ג, א-ב.
80. שם, כלל ד, ט.
81. שם, כלל ה, ב-ד.
82. שם, ובהלכה ה.
83. שם.
84. שם, הלכה ז.
85. שם, הלכה ה.
86. שם, הלכה א.
87. שם, כלל ח, י.
88. שם.
89. שם, כלל ט, ה.
90. שם, כלל ח, ג. ובהלכות רכילות ז, ב ובבאמ"ח שם ס"ק ב.
91. שם, הלכה ב.
92. ויקרא יט, טז.
93. עי' מדרש תנחומא פרשת פקודי. ובמדרש רבה, דברים (פ' כי תצא) פ"ט, וברד"ל שם
94. ראה שערי תשובה לרבנו יונה, שער שלישי אות רה. וע' שבט מוסר פרק כא; יערות דבש, דרוש טו.
95. רמב"ם הלכות דעות ז, א. ח"ח הלכות רכילות כלל א, א.
96. ח"ח שם ג, ג.
97. ח"ח שם א, ב.
98. ראה הערה הבאה.
99. וז"ל רבנו יונה ב'שערי תשובה' שער שלישי, אות רכב: "ונזק הרכילות חדל לספור כי אין מספר, **כי הוא מרבה שנאה בעולם**".
100. ח"ח הלכות רכילות כלל ח, ב.
101. שם ח, ד. ובבאמ"ח ס"ק ו.
102. עי' בהקדמה לספר שמירת הלשון.
103. 'זכור למרים' פרק ד.

104. הובא בספר 'שאל אביל ויגדך' מהג"ר שלום שוואדראן זצ"ל ששמע את הסיפור מהג"ר משה אהרן שטערן זצ"ל, משגיח דישיבת קאמעניץ בירושלים ת"ו, ששמעו בבחרותו מהג"ר יעקב קאמענעצקי זצ"ל.
105. הג"ר שלום זצ"ל ידע מי ה' הגדול השני.
106. ראה שמירת הלשון, שער התבונה פרק ה: "וכאשר נתבונן באמת, נמצא **שקיום מצות לדון את חברו לכף זכות ומדת שמירת ומדת שמירת הלשון תלויים בקיום מצות עשה של "ואהבת לרעך כמוך"** (ויקרא יט, יח). שאם יאהב את חברו באמת, בודאי באמת, בודאי לא ידבר עליו לשון הרע, ויחפש עליו בכל כוחותיו זכות". ועיין שם מה שהביא מדברי הרמב"ם (הלכות אבלות יד, א) שמצוות ואהבת לרעך כמוך הוא שיחוס על ממון וכבוד חברו כמו שהוא חושש על ממונו וכבוד עצמו.
107. עי' 'זכור למרים' פרק יא.
108. ראה בס' המאורות הגדולים מה שאמר פעם החפץ חיים זצ"ל הנדיבים הידועים במאסקווא שכשצריכים לכתוב מברק, מדקדקים מאוד בניסוח המברק כדי שלא יעלה הרבה כסף, לפי שצריכים לשלם על כל מלה ומלה. ואם בעניני הנוגעים לעניני כסף בלבד מדקדקים הבריות כל כך, כמה צריכים לדקדק ולספור כל מלה, כשזה נוגע לאיסורים חמורים, ופוגע בהפסדי ממונות וגם בדיני נפשות...".
109. חפץ חיים בהקדמה; חובת השמירה פרק ג; שמירת הלשון שער התבונה פרק טו. ועי' במכתבו של הג"ר איסר זלמן מלצר זצ"ל, בראש ספר 'עקרי דינים' לר"ש הומינר זצ"ל.
110. חפץ חיים בהקדמה.
111. ראה בארוכה שמירת הלשון שער התבונה פרק טו, וזכור למרים פרק יד.
112. שמירת הלשון שער התבונה פרק ג. וע' מועד קטן ה, ב. וראה בס' חפץ חיים על התורה עמ' קיז, סיפור עם הגה"צ ר' נפתלי זילברברג זצ"ל מווארשא.
113. ראה שערי תשובה לרבנו יונה, שער שני אות ל: "ואמרו המוסרים: ההרגל על כל דבר נעשה שלטון". ועי' יומא פו,א.
114. ויותר מזה כתב מרן בעל חפץ חיים זצ"ל בס' שמירת הלשון ח"ב פרק ז (פרשת כי תבוא) ובכבוד שמים פ"ב, וז"ל שם: "ובאמת לפלא הוא בעיני, שטבע בני האדם לחפש סגולות וברכות מאנשים גדולים להצלחה על פרנסה, ומה יועילו להם כל הסגולות והברכות, אם חס ושלום הוא מורגל בזה החטא של לשון הרע ורכילות... **ואם היו שומעים לדברי, הייתי מיעץ להם שישמרו עצמם בזהירות יתירה מזה החטא... שאז בודאי יתברכו נכסיהם יותר מכל הסגולות**".
115. הלכות רכילות כלל ה, א.
116. הלכות לשה"ר כלל ז.
117. הלכות לשה"ר כלל ו, א.
118. הג"ר מנחם מענדל זאקס זצ"ל בהקדמתו לס' "חפץ חיים", העיד בשם חותנו מרן החפץ חיים זצ"ל, "שרוב העולם משקרין, וכולם מגזימים, ואין להאמינם".
119. ראה באמ"ח בפתיחה עשין ג ס"ק ג, ד"ה ומה שכתבנו.
120. עי' באמ"ח הלכות לשה"ר כלל ו, ס"ק ב ד"ה וחפשתי.

[ב]

121. הלכות לשה"ר כלל ז, ו. ועי' באמ"ח, הלכות לשה"ר כלל א ס"ק טולגבי ישעי' הנביא. ובאמ"ח שם כלל ב סוף ס"ק ג.
122. הלכות לשה"ר כלל ז, י-יג. ועיין שם בריש כלל ז' עוד כמה פרטים ותנאים בזה. ויש עוד מקרים מסויימים שמותר לקבל, כמבואר שם, ולא הבאנום כאן יען כי רבו הפרטים, ואין זו מטרת החיבור.

123. כנ"ל הערה 137.
124. ראה רמב"ם הלכות דעות, פרק ז הלכה ו. פתיחה, עשין ו. הלכות לשה"ר כלל ט, ד.
125. הלכות לשה"ר כלל א, ז.
126. פשוט.
127. הלכות לשה"ר כלל ו, ה פרט ג.
128. שם, הלכה ו.
129. שם, הלכה ה.
130. שם.
131. שם.
132. שם.
133. ראה לעיל הערה 118 מה שהעיד הג"ר מנחם מענדל זאקס זצ"ל בהקדמתו לס' "חפץ חיים", בשם חותנו מרן החפץ חיים זצ"ל, "שרוב העולם משקרין, וכולם מגזימים, ואין להאמינם".
134. רמב"ם, ספר המצוות עשין קעז. שערי תשובה לרבנו יונה, שער שלישי אות ריח.
135. ראה באמ"ח פתיחה עשין ג, סק"ג.
136. ספר אור לציון – עבודה מאמר ז.
137. מדרש רבה, במדבר ט, ז.
138. דברים יד, א. וראה שמות ד, כב.
139. הלכות רכילות, כלל ט, א.
140. שם, הלכה ב, תנאי ג.
141. ויקרא יט, טז.
142. שם, באמ"ח ס"ק א.
143. שם, הלכה א.
144. שם, הלכה ג.
145. הלכות לשה"ר כלל ו, יא. הלכות רכילות כלל ט, ב תנאי ה.
146. הלכות רכילות כלל ט, ב תנאי ד.
147. ע"פ אבות דר' נתן. (ויש בזה חילוקי דעות בחז"ל אם מרים דיברה בפני משה או שלא בפניו).
148. הלכות לשה"ר כלל ד, ה.
149. הלכות לשה"ר כלל ד, יא וכלל ו, ב ע"פ הגמ' בנדה סא, א: "אמר רבא: האי לישנא בישא אע"פ דלקבולי לא מבעי, מיחש לי' מבעי".
150. הלכות לשה"ר כלל ד, ג. וכל זה לענין להאמין ולקבל בעינן תרי, אבל לחוש אפילו בעד אחד סגי אם לא יחסרו הפרטים הנ"ל.
151. בספר חפץ חיים הביא עוד כמה תנאים, ובתוכם שיתכוין אך ורק להצלתו של חבירו ולא בשביל חשבונות שלו (ראה ח"ח הל' לשה"ר כלל י' והל' רכילות כלל ט').
152. באמ"ח, הלכות לשה"ר, כלל ד ס"ק מח.
153. הלכות לשה"ר, כלל ד, יב.
154. הלכות לשה"ר, כלל ו, ט. שמירת הלשון, שער הזכירה פרק יג.
155. שמירת הלשון, ח"ב פ"ז.
156. כבוד שמים, פרק ג.
157. חובת השמירה, פרק ח. זכור למרים, פרק כה. וראה ב'שמירת הלשון' שער התבונה, פרק ב מה שהביא מאגרת הגר"א זצ"ל, וז"ל: ועד יום מותו צריך האדם ליסר את עצמו, ולא בתענית וסיגופים, כי אם ברסן פיו ובתאותיו, וזהו התשובה . . . **ו ז ה ו**

יותר מכל התעניתים וסגופים שבעולם ...". והביא החח"ח שם מספר 'ראש הגבעה' שכשאדם רוצה להתנדב תענית, טוב יותר שיקבל עליו התענית מן הדיבור, ממה שיקבל עליו מן האכילה, כי ממנו לא יהיק לו נזק, לא בגופו ולא בנשמתו, ולא יחלש על ידי התענית הזה."

158. שמירת הלשון, שער התבונה, פרק ח. וראה בסוף ספר 'שמירת הלשון' דברים נפלאים בענין זה.
159. עי' זוה"ק במדבר קפג.
160. עי' לעיל בהקדמה, לגבי דורו של אחאב, ובהערות שם.
161. עי' לעיל הערה 16.
162. מדרש שיר השירים א. מדרש תנחומא, וירא ח. וע' זוה"ק בראשית רנד.
163. עי' חובת השמירה, פרק ח: "לפי מה שבררנו את גודל הענין של קבלת השמירה, אפילו באיש פרטי שמקבל על עצמו, וכל שכן כמה גדולה קדושת הענין כשתתמצא חבורה בענין זה, שיתחזקו לכבוד השי"ת לעשות סייג בעצמם לשמור את כח הדיבור שלא ידברו דברים האסורים. כמה נחת רוח יגיע להקב"ה מזה, כשרואה שחביבים מצוותיו לישראל, וכל מצוה ומצוה תלמד זכות עליהם."
164. שמירת הלשון, שער התבונה פרק ב בשם הגר"א באגרת 'עלים לתרופה'. (וכ"כ בס' ראש הגבעה) שכשאדם רוצה להתנדב תענית, טוב יותר לקבל ע"ע תענית מן הדיבור מלקבל ע"ע תענית מן האכילה, כי בתענית דיבור לא יהי' לו נזק לא בגופו ולא בנשמתו וכו' ע"ש.
165. בזוהר חדש (סוף פרשת נח) כנישתא חדא דיתערון בתיובתא וכו', ע"ש.

Part Three

166. עי' תענית כה, א.
167. ראה לדוגמא בתפלת 'היום הרת עולם' במוסף לר"ה: "אם כבנים... ואם כעבדים...".
168. תנא דבי אליהו, פרק כח: בני אהובי, כלום חסרתי דבר שאבקש מכם? ומה אני מבקש מכם? אלא שתהיו אוהבין זה את זה, ותהיו מכבדין זה את זה. ראה שמירת הלשון, שער התבונה פרק ה.
169. סנהדרין ק, א.
170. עי' אהבת חסד ח"ב, פרק ה ובהגהה שם. זכור למרים פרק יא.
171. ראה מדרש תנחומא, שמות כה.
172. ויקרא יט, טז.
173. עי' ראש השנה כט, א.
174. בבא קמא צב, א: "כל המבקש רחמים על חברו, והוא צריך לאותו דבר, הוא נענה תחילה."
175. שמות ו, ה.
176. בפירושו על התורה (שם).
177. ראה גם באהבת חסד ח"ג פרק ח.
178. ז"ל רבינו יונה שם (בעמ' קעא): "שמעת צרת ישראל הרחוקים, היאנח והתפלל עליהם, וכל שכן על הקרובים". ושם (בעמ' קפד) כתב: "ויתפלל בכל יום כפי צחות לשונו על כל חולי בני ישראל שיתרפאו, ועל הבריאים שלא יחלו, ושינצלו מכל נזק, ושיציל הקב"ה את בני ישראל מכל גויים... ושישיב ליראתו כל האנוסים ביד הגויים... ועל כולם,

שישמור הקב"ה שארית עמו, וינקום את נקמתם במהרה בימינו, ועל עם הקודש שישובו בתשובה שלימה, ויקבלם ויחזירם בתשובה שלימה לפניו".
179. 'שמעת צרת ישראל הרחוקים' – הכוונה יכול להיות גם על אלה הרחוקים בריחוק מקום וגם על אלה הרחוקים בנפש וברוח.

ACHDUS PRAYER

Master of the universe, My Father, My King!

I declare before You that I have been truly blind. I have treated Your commandments as a burden and did not understand their great power and benefit, that is, that they have the power to attach me to You as nothing else can, and that this attachment is my entry to an eternity with You. I have been blind to the great gift of Your mercy and especially to the power of repentance and its ability to erase my transgressions as if they never occurred.

Woe is me that I have not taken advantage of such a gift. Having failed to repent, my blindness has further aggravated my situation by allowing me to become my own worst enemy. I have slandered my fellow Jew and in so doing, I have empowered Satan, the great accuser, to examine my transgressions before the eyes of Justice rather than before the eyes of Mercy. Even worse is what my slander has done to my fellow Jew in that it has opened an evil eye upon him and forced him before the eyes of Justice as well.

If I had only known the deadly power of my mouth!!

I pray with all my heart that it is not too late for him. If I have slandered him, it is only because of my smallness and petty jealousies, but G-d forbid, that through it, I should cause him any harm. I sincerely disallow my human frailties to empower accusations against him in the heavenly court of Justice.

Perhaps worst of all, my blindness has prevented me from seeing one of Your greatest truths, that every Jew, whoever and wherever he is, is in reality my brother and sister and that we are one family before You, our eternal Father. How could I have been so blind and not seen it from Your perspective.

I have treated my brother as a stranger and even sometimes as an enemy. I have allowed the legitimate differences of nationality or religious customs which existed between us to become the reason for real separation and division. In my arrogance, I felt superior to my brother, and treated him accordingly, never seeing his pain and Your profound disappointment.

How could I have thought that treating my brother as an inferior would meet with Your approval and bring me closer to You?? How could I have ignored the pain that a Father has when he sees his children treat each other with mutual contempt?? Even when I justifiably disagreed with my brother, I should have prayed for him, not slandered or denigrated him. Woe is a brother who is blind to the pain of a brother. Woe is a son who is blind to the pain of his Father. I declare before You, however, that I am no longer blind. I have awakened and I see with a new vision, Your vision.

Yet, ironically, this new vision brings me great pain. For the first time, I truly see my brother's suffering and agony and I truly feel his danger. Now, I sincerely cry out for my brother as a brother, and I ask You to listen to me as the Father of us both. Save my brother and redeem him for his danger is great!!

To see my brother in his crisis, to see him enter through the door of tragedy and catastrophe is an unbearable sight. How am I to live with it? From where shall it take the strength? My heart bleeds to see the eventual disappearance of millions of my brothers and sisters worldwide to the twin plagues of assimilation and intermarriage. How can I bear to see so many lost brothers and sisters, souls lost to their Father in Heaven? Are they not the descendants of Abraham? Were they not present, as souls, at the revelation at Sinai? Are they not my family? Are You not their Father?

Save them, I beseech You, before it is too late. Bestow upon them a new light through which they can clearly recognize their Father in Heaven. To witness the destruction of my Jewish brothers and sisters in the land of Israel is unbearable. To even see this as a possibility is extremely painful. How I feel the pain and terror of my brothers who live there. Here, where I reside, I feel safe, but how can I have any peace of mind? Can I be safe when my brothers are in danger?

Save my brothers and sisters from the evil *Yishmael, Esav,* and the *Eirev Rav.* Restore Your presence to Zion, my Father, and let Your children rejoice in Your palace.

Restrain Your anger from those who are closest to You, those who observe Your Torah. How many of their young must die? How many orphans must they count? How much sickness must they bear? Has their cup not been filled? True, they should have known better. They should have felt Your pain and that of all their brothers and sisters. They bear greater responsibility because they have the power to redeem Your children. Have compassion on them. Open their eyes and let them see the pain of a Father. They are Your most loyal ones.

Listen to the cry of brother for his brothers.

Please hear me as our Father. Redeem them because they are Your children. Listen to my outcry for the sake of my forefathers, Abraham, Isaac, and Israel, Your servants, to whom You promised a redemption for their children. Listen to my cry for the sake of Rachel, our Mother. Has there even been a greater sister than Rachel who would give up her beloved Jacob for her sister's sake so that she could protect her from embarrassment?

Has there ever been a greater mother than Rachel who prayed and wept for her children long after she left their presence?

Listen to my cry for the sake of the Jews who left Egypt and who followed their Father in Heaven into an unknown wilderness simply because He was their Father. Has there even been demonstrated a more trusting children than when they accepted Your will as a Father by saying, "Na'aseh" before "Nishma", "We will do" even before "we understand"? Listen to my cry for the sake of the righteous Jews of all generations whose only thought was to give You nachas from Your children. Listen to my cry for the sake of all the Jews who suffered and died from Your Name's sake because they knew that while one can renounce a king, on can never renounce a Father.

If my brothers and sisters are in danger, I do not criticize You for it because Your actions are just and perfect. Yet, I must tell You of my pain and plead with You to reverse Yourself. Be our Father first and our King second. Show mercy and compassion first and justice only second. If we cry to You as children, a brother for a brother, shall you not, measure for measure, respond to us as a Father and not as a King?

Let there be an awakening from below. Let my family, the Jewish people, ultimately come near to You by virtue of their suffering and the deaths of their saintly ones. **Grant us the strength to earn Your presence, once and for all, with heads held high.**

Grant us the leadership which is appropriate for this task. Let us be worthy of the light You wish to grant us and let us achieve true peace in this world and in the next.

Amen, may it be Your will.

תְּפִלַּת הָאָח

המהדורה השלמה

אָבִינוּ מַלְכֵּנוּ, בָּאנוּ לְהִתְחַנֵּן וּלְהִתְוַדּוֹת לְפָנֶיךָ עַל שֶׁזֶּה כַּמָּה שָׁנִים טָחוּ עֵינֵינוּ מֵרְאוֹת אֶת הָאֱמֶת, וּכְעִוְרִים הַמְגַשְּׁשִׁים בָּאֲפֵלָה נִדְמֵינוּ. מֵרֹב עָוֹנֵינוּ הָיָה לָנוּ הַתּוֹרָה וְהַמִּצְווֹת לְטֹרַח וּלְמַשָּׂא, וְלֹא רָאִינוּ מָה רַב חֵילָם וּשְׂכָרָם בֶּאֱמֶת, דְּהַיְנוּ שֶׁיֵּשׁ בָּהֶם - וְרַק בָּהֶם - הַכֹּחַ לְקָרֵב אוֹתָנוּ וּלְדַבְּקֵנוּ אֵלֶיךָ, וְשֶׁדְּבֵקוּת זוֹ תִּתֵּן לָנוּ הַזְּכוּת לְהִכָּנֵס אִתְּךָ לְאַפִּרְיוֹן מְחִיצָתְךָ לְנֶצַח נְצָחִים.

כְּעִוְרִים נְגַשֵּׁשׁ וְנֵלֵךְ וְלֹא רָאִינוּ הַמַּתָּנוֹת הַגְּדוֹלוֹת שֶׁחֲנַנְתָּ אוֹתָנוּ בְּמִדַּת רַחֲמֶיךָ, וּבִפְרָט הַמַּתָּנָה טוֹבָה שֶׁל תְּשׁוּבָה, אֲשֶׁר בְּכוֹחָהּ וּבִיכָלְתָּהּ לִמְחוֹת כְּעָב פְּשָׁעֵינוּ וְכֶעָנָן חַטֹּאתֵינוּ, וּכְאִלּוּ לֹא עֲשִׂינוּם מֵעוֹלָם. אוֹי וַאֲבוֹי לָנוּ שֶׁלֹּא נִצַּלְנוּ מַתָּנָה יְקָרָה זוֹ. לֹא דַּי שֶׁלֹּא חָזַרְנוּ בִּתְשׁוּבָה אֶלָּא הָעִוָּרוֹן שֶׁלָּנוּ הוֹרִידָנוּ מַטָּה מַטָּה עַד שֶׁנֶּהֱפַכְנוּ לְאוֹיְבֵנוּ הַגָּדוֹל בְּיוֹתֵר.

הָלַכְנוּ רָכִיל וְדִבַּרְנוּ לָשׁוֹן הָרַע עַל בְּנֵי עַמֵּנוּ, וּבָזֶה נָתַנּוּ כֹּחַ וָעֹז לַשָּׂטָן, הַמְקַטְרֵג הַגָּדוֹל, לְהָבִיא צְרוֹר חֲטָאֵינוּ וּפְשָׁעֵינוּ לִפְנֵי כִּסֵּא הַדִּין שֶׁבְּבֵית דִּינְךָ הַצֶּדֶק, וְלֹא לִפְנֵי כִּסֵּא הָרַחֲמִים, וְנִתְקַיֵּם בָּנוּ מִקְרָא שֶׁכָּתוּב (משלי יח, ז) "פִּי כְסִיל מְחִתָּה לוֹ, וּשְׂפָתָיו מוֹקֵשׁ נַפְשׁוֹ", וְלֹא זָכִינוּ לַחֲנִינָתְךָ בְּרַחֲמֶיךָ הָרַבִּים וְלִשְׁמִירָתְךָ הָעֶלְיוֹנָה מִמִּדַּת הַדִּין הַתַּקִּיפָה, וּכְמוֹ שֶׁכָּתוּב (שם כא, כג) "שֹׁמֵר פִּיו וּלְשׁוֹנוֹ - שֹׁמֵר מִצָּרוֹת נַפְשׁוֹ", וְלָכֵן צָרוֹת רַבּוֹת סְבָבוּנוּ, כִּי עֲווֹנוֹתֵינוּ וּפְשָׁעֵנוּ הַשָּׂטָן רִגּוּ, עָלוּ עַל צַוָּארֵנוּ הִכְשִׁילוּ כֹחֵנוּ.

עוֹד רָעָה גְדוֹלָה מִזוֹ הִיא מַה שֶׁגָּרְמָה הַלָּשׁוֹן הָרַע שֶׁלָּנוּ לַחֲבֵרֵינוּ, שֶׁשָּׂמְנוּ עָלָיו עַיִן רָעָה, וּבְזֶה הִכְרַחְנוּ גַּם אוֹתוֹ לַעֲמוֹד לִפְנֵי כִּסֵּא הַדִּין. הַלְוַאי וְיָדַעְנוּ כֹּחַ הָאֶרֶס שֶׁבְּפִינוּ וּלְשׁוֹנֵנוּ וְשֶׁהַמָּוֶת וְהַחַיִּים בְּיַד הַלָּשׁוֹן (ע"פ משלי יח, כא).

בְּכָל זֹאת הִנְנוּ מִתְחַנְּנִים לְפָנֶיךָ, וּמְקוֹמוֹת אָנוּ בְּכָל לֵב שֶׁלֹּא אִיחַרְנוּ הַמּוֹעֵד. אִם דִּבַּרְנוּ עָלָיו לָשׁוֹן הָרַע וּרְכִילוּת הֲרֵי זֶה רַק מֵחֲמַת קַטְנוּתֵנוּ וְקִנְאַת אִישׁ מֵרֵעֵהוּ, אֲבָל חַס וְחָלִילָה שֶׁיִּיגָּרֵם לַחֲבֵרֵנוּ שׁוּם נֵזֶק עַל יָדֵינוּ כְּלָל. וְהִנְנוּ מוֹסְרִים מוֹדָעָה וְאָנוּ מְבַקְּשִׁים בְּכָל לֵב שֶׁלֹּא יוֹסִיפוּ קַטְנוּתֵנוּ וְקוֹצֶר הַשָּׂגָתֵנוּ שׁוּם כֹּחַ וְעֹז לְעוֹרֵר בַּמְּרוֹמִים אֵיזוֹ תְּבִיעָה כְּנֶגְדּוֹ בְּבֵית דִּין שֶׁל מַעְלָה.

הַדָּבָר הַגָּרוּעַ בְּיוֹתֵר שֶׁעוֹלֵל לָנוּ הָעִוָּרוֹן הוּא שֶׁזֶּה מָנַע מִמֶּנּוּ הַהַכָּרָה בְּאַחַת מִן הָאֲמִתִּיּוֹת הַגְּדוֹלוֹת שֶׁבָּעוֹלָם: **שֶׁכָּל יְהוּדִי וִיהוּדִי, יִהְיֶה מִי שֶׁיִּהְיֶה וּבְאֵיזֶה מַצָּב שֶׁיִּהְיֶה, הוּא בֶּאֱמֶת אָחִי וַאֲחוֹתִי, בָּשָׂר מִבְּשָׂרִי, וְשֶׁכּוּלָּנוּ בְּנֵי מִשְׁפָּחָה אַחַת בְּעֵינֶיךָ, אָבִינוּ שֶׁבַּשָּׁמַיִם.** אֵיךְ נִסְתְּמוּ עֵינֵינוּ כָּל כָּךְ וְלֹא רָאִינוּ הַדְּבָרִים מֵהַשְׁקָפָתְךָ אַתָּה.

הִתְיַחַסְנוּ אֶל אָחִינוּ כְּאֶל אִישׁ זָר, וְלִפְעָמִים אַף כְּאֶל אוֹיֵב. נָתַנּוּ לְחִילוּקֵי הַמִּנְהָגִים שֶׁהָיָה בֵּינֵינוּ, וְהִשְׁתַּיְּכוּיוֹתֵנוּ לְפִי אַרְצוֹת מוֹצָאֵינוּ לִהְיוֹת סִיבָּה לְפֵרוּד לְבָבוֹת אֲמִתִּי. בְּגַאֲוָתֵנוּ, הִרְגַּשְׁנוּ עֶלְיוֹנוּת עָלָיו וְלָכֵן הִתְיַחַסְנוּ אֵלָיו בְּגַאֲוָה וָבוּז, וְלֹא רָאִינוּ בְּצַעֲרוֹ וְלֹא הִשְׁגַּחְנוּ עַל גּוֹדֶל הַכְּאֵב שֶׁלְּךָ. אֵיךְ עָלָה בִּכְלָל עַל דַּעְתֵּנוּ שֶׁיַּחַס כָּזֶה עִם אָחִינוּ יְקָרֵב אוֹתָנוּ אֵלֶיךָ? אֵיךְ הִתְעַלַּמְנוּ מֵהַכְּאֵב שֶׁיֵּשׁ לוֹ לְאָב בִּרְאוֹתוֹ גּוֹדֶל הַשִּׂנְאָה בְּלֵב בָּנָיו, הָאֶחָד עַל הַשֵּׁנִי?.

אפילו כְּשֶׁחָלַקְנוּ עַל אָחִינוּ בְּצֶדֶק, הָיָה לָנוּ לְהִתְפַּלֵּל בַּעֲדוֹ שֶׁיִּרְאֶה אֶת אוֹר הָאֱמֶת, וְלֹא לְדַבֵּר עָלָיו לְשׁוֹן הָרַע וּלְהַשְׁפִּילוֹ עַד לֶעָפָר. אוֹי לוֹ לְאָח שֶׁעֵינָיו סְתוּמוֹת מִלְּהַרְגִּישׁ בְּצַעַר אָחִיו, וְאוֹי לוֹ לְבֵן שֶׁעֵינָיו סְתוּמוֹת מִלִּרְאוֹת בְּצַעַר אָבִיו.

אָמְנָם בָּאנוּ לוֹמַר לְפָנֶיךָ שֶׁנִּפְקְחוּ עֵינֵינוּ כְּבָר, וְהָעִוָּרוֹן שֶׁלָּנוּ חָלַף הָלַךְ לוֹ. הִתְעוֹרַרְנוּ מִתַּרְדֵּמָתֵנוּ, וּמֵעַתָּה אָנוּ מַבִּיטִים עַל אַחֵינוּ בְּנֵי יִשְׂרָאֵל בְּהַשְׁקָפָה חֲדָשָׁה - הַהַשְׁקָפָה שֶׁלְּךָ! אָמְנָם מֻכְרָחִים אָנוּ לוֹמַר שֶׁהַהַשְׁקָפָה זוֹ גּוֹרֶמֶת לָנוּ הַרְבֵּה צַעַר וְעַגְמַת נֶפֶשׁ. כִּי זֹאת הַפַּעַם הָרִאשׁוֹנָה שֶׁאָנוּ רוֹאִים בֶּאֱמֶת אֶת צַעֲרוֹ וּכְאֵבוֹ שֶׁל אָחִינוּ וְאָנוּ מַרְגִּישִׁים בְּסַכָּנוֹת הָאִיּוּמוֹת שֶׁהוּא שָׁרוּי בָּהּ. וְעַתָּה אָבִינוּ, אָב רַחוּם וְחַנּוּן, הִנֶּנּוּ בֶּאֱמֶת שׁוֹפְכִים לְפָנֶיךָ לֵב כַּמַּיִם וְצוֹעֲקִים לְמַעַן אָחִינוּ כְּאָח הַמַּרְגִּישׁ וּמִצְטַעֵר בְּצַעַר אָחִיו, וְאָנוּ מְבַקְשִׁים מִמְּךָ שֶׁתִּשְׁמַע וּתְקַבֵּל צַעֲקָתֵנוּ, שֶׁהֲרֵי אַתָּה הָאַבָּא שֶׁל שְׁנֵינוּ. הַצֵּל נָא אֶת אָחִינוּ וּפְדֵה אוֹתוֹ מִכָּל צָרוֹתָיו בְּעוֹד מוֹעֵד, כִּי הוּא בְּצָרָה גְּדוֹלָה מְאֹד. אֵין אָנוּ יְכוֹלִים לִסְבֹּל בִּרְאוֹתֵנוּ אֶת אָחִינוּ בְּמַצָּב סַכָּנָה כְּשֶׁהוּא עוֹמֵד בְּגֵיא צַלְמָוֶת וּבְשַׁעֲרֵי הַהֶרֶס וְהַחֻרְבָּן. אֵיךְ נוּכַל לִחְיוֹת עִם זֶה? מֵאַיִן נִשְׁאָב הַכֹּחַ לָזֶה?

לְמַעַן אַחַ"י שֶׁהִתְעָרְבוּ בַּגּוֹיִים:

לִבֵּנוּ מֵיצַר וְדוֹאֵב, בִּרְאוֹתֵנוּ בְּאָבְדָן מִלְיוֹנֵי אַחֵינוּ בְּנֵי יִשְׂרָאֵל בְּכָל קַצְוֵי תֵּבֵל - וּבִפְרָט בִּמְדִינַת אָמֶרִיקָה - לְמַכַּת הַהִתְבּוֹלְלוּת וְנִשּׂוּאֵי תַּעֲרוּבֶת, רַחֲמָנָא לִצְּלָן. אֵיךְ נוּכַל לִרְאוֹת בְּאָבְדָן כָּל כָּךְ הַרְבֵּה אַחִים וַאֲחָיוֹת, נְשָׁמוֹת אוֹבְדוֹת לַאֲבִיהֶם שֶׁבַּשָּׁמַיִם. וְכִי לֹא מִזֶּרַע אַבְרָהָם יִצְחָק וְיַעֲקֹב הֵם? הַאִם לֹא הָיוּ נִשְׁמוֹתֵיהֶם נוֹכְחוֹת בְּשָׁעָה שֶׁנִּגְלֵיתָ עַל הַר סִינַי וְהִשְׁמַעְתָּ מִתּוֹךְ הָאֵשׁ: 'אָנֹכִי ה' אֱלֹקֶיךָ'? וְכִי לֹאו בְּנֵי מִשְׁפַּחְתֵּנוּ הֵם? הַאִם אֵינְךָ אֲבִיהֶם? אָנָּא הַצֵּל אוֹתָם

בְּעוֹד מוֹעֵד, חוּשָׁה נָא וְאַל תְּאַחַר. תָּעֶרֶה עֲלֵיהֶם רוּחַ מִמָּרוֹם כְּדֵי שֶׁיּוּכְלוּ לְהַכִּיר בְּבֵרוּר מִי הוּא אֲבִיהֶם שֶׁבַּשָּׁמַיִם.

למען אחב"י בארה"ק:

אֵין אָנוּ יְכוֹלִים לִחְיוֹת בִּמְנוּחָה וּבְשַׁלְוָה בִּמְקוֹמוֹת מוֹשְׁבוֹתֵינוּ בִּתְפוּצוֹת הַגּוֹלָה בְּשָׁעָה שֶׁאַחֵינוּ בְּנֵי יִשְׂרָאֵל תּוֹשָׁבֵי אֶרֶץ הַקּוֹדֶשׁ חַיִּים בִּדְאָגָה וּבַחֲרָדָה מִדֵּי יוֹם בְּיוֹמוֹ מִפַּחַד הָאוֹיְבִים, זֶרַע יִשְׁמָעֵאל, הָאוֹרְבִים לְחַיֵּיהֶם תָּמִיד. אֵיךְ נִמְצָא מַרְגּוֹעַ לְנַפְשֵׁנוּ כָּאן כְּשֶׁאַחֵינוּ וְאַחְיוֹתֵינוּ מוּקָּפִים מְאוֹיְבִים צְמֵאֵי דָּם הַמִּתְיַעֲצִים עֲלֵיהֶם לְהַכְחִידָם וְלֹא יִזָּכֵר שֵׁם יִשְׂרָאֵל עוֹד, חָלִילָה. אָנָּא הַצֵּל אוֹתָם בְּעוֹד מוֹעֵד מֵהַיָּדַיִם הָאַכְזָרִיִּים שֶׁל זֶרַע יִשְׁמָעֵאל, עֵשָׂו וְהָעֵרֶב רַב. הָשֵׁב שְׁכִינָתְךָ לְצִיּוֹן עִירֶךָ וְיַחְזְרוּ בָּנֶיךָ לְשֻׁלְחַן אֲבִיהֶם.

למען אחב"י שומרי תורה ומצוות:

הָשֵׁב כַּעַסְךָ וַחֲרוֹן אַפְּךָ מִבָּנֶיךָ שׁוֹמְרֵי תּוֹרָתֶךָ וּמִצְוֹתֶיךָ, הַקְּרוֹבִים אֵלֶיךָ בְּיוֹתֵר. אָנָּא, אַל יָמוּתוּ צְעִירֵיהֶם בִּדְמֵי יְמֵיהֶם. כַּמָּה יְתוֹמִים צְרִיכִים הֵם לִמְנוֹת? כַּמָּה חוֹלִים צְרִיכִים הֵם לִסְבֹּל? הַאִם לֹא נִתְמַלֵּא כְּבָר כּוֹס צָרָתָם? אֱמֶת וְנָכוֹן שֶׁהָאַחֲרָיוּת רוֹבֶצֶת עֲלֵיהֶם בְּיוֹתֵר, כִּי לָהֶם הַיִּתְרוֹן שֶׁל יְדִיעַת הַתּוֹרָה וְגַם הַכֹּחַ לִפְדּוֹת שְׁאָר בָּנֶיךָ שֶׁאֵינָם יוֹדְעִים מְאוּמָה וּלְהָאִיר אֶת אוֹרְךָ עֲלֵיהֶם. אַךְ אָנָּא רַחֵם עֲלֵיהֶם כִּי הֵם בָּשָׂר וָדָם. אָנָּא פְּתַח עֵינֵיהֶם וְתֵן לָהֶם לִרְאוֹת בְּצַעֲרוֹ שֶׁל הָאָב. הֲלֹא הֵמָּה בָּנֶיךָ וִידִידֶיךָ הַנֶּאֱמָנִים לְךָ בְּיוֹתֵר.

שְׁמַע נָא לְקוֹל זַעֲקַת הָאָח בְּעַד אָחִיו. אָנָּא שְׁמַע קוֹלֵנוּ כְּאָבִינוּ. הַקְשִׁיבָה לְקוֹל שַׁוְעָתֵנוּ. עֲשֵׂה לְמַעַן אֲבוֹתֵינוּ אַבְרָהָם יִצְחָק וְיִשְׂרָאֵל עֲבָדֶיךָ שֶׁמֵּאַהֲבָתְךָ שֶׁאָהַבְתָּ אוֹתָם הִבְטַחְתָּ לָהֶם שֶׁתָּבִיא גְּאוּלָה לִבְנֵי בְּנֵיהֶם.

עננו בִּזְכוּת רָחֵל אִמֵּנוּ שֶׁמֵּרוֹב אַהֲבָתָהּ וּרְגִישׁוּתָהּ לְמַעַן לֵאָה אֲחוֹתָהּ הָיְתָה מוּכֶנֶת לְוַתֵּר עַל בַּעְלָהּ הַצַּדִּיק, יַעֲקֹב אָבִינוּ, וּלְאַבֵּד לָנֶצַח הַזְּכוּת לְהַעֲמִיד אֶת הַשְּׁבָטִים, שֶׁהֵם עַמּוּדֵי הָעוֹלָם שִׁבְטֵי יָ-הּ, וְכָל זֶה כְּדֵי לִמְנוֹעַ בּוּשָׁה וְצַעַר מֵאֲחוֹתָהּ הַגְּדוֹלָה. הַאִם יֵשׁ אֵם רַחֲמָנִיָּה וְאוֹהֶבֶת יוֹתֵר מֵרָחֵל אִמֵּנוּ שֶׁהִתְפַּלְּלָה וּבָכְתָה עַל בָּנֶיהָ יָמִים רַבִּים לְאַחַר שֶׁנִּסְתַּלְּקָה מֵהֶם?

עננו בִּזְכוּת אֲבוֹתֵינוּ שֶׁהָלְכוּ אַחֲרֶיךָ בַּמִּדְבָּר בְּאֶרֶץ לֹא זְרוּעָה, אַךְ וְרַק בִּשְׁבִיל שֶׁאַתָּה אֲבִיהֶם. עֲנֵנוּ בִּזְכוּת בָּנֶיךָ שֶׁהוֹכִיחוּ אֶת בִּטְחוֹנָם בַּאֲבִיהֶם בְּשָׁעָה שֶׁעָמְדוּ לִפְנֵי הַר סִינַי וְהִקְדִּימוּ 'נַעֲשֶׂה' לְ'נִשְׁמָע' וְקִיבְּלוּ עֲלֵיהֶם וְעַל זַרְעָם לַעֲשׂוֹת רְצוֹן אֲבִיהֶם כְּבָנִים נֶאֱמָנִים. עֲנֵנוּ בִּזְכוּת צַדִּיקֵי הַדּוֹרוֹת שֶׁכָּל מַחְשְׁבוֹתָם וּמְגַמָּתָם הָיְתָה רַק לְהָבִיא לְפָנֶיךָ נַחַת רוּחַ מִבָּנֶיךָ אֲהוּבֶיךָ. עֲנֵנוּ לְמַעַן קְדוֹשִׁים מֻשְׁלָכִים בָּאֵשׁ עַל קִדּוּשׁ שְׁמֶךָ, אֲשֶׁר יָדְעוּ שֶׁאַף עַל פִּי שֶׁבְּנֵי הַמְּדִינָה יְכוֹלִים לִפְרוֹק מֵעֲלֵיהֶם עֻלּוֹ שֶׁל מֶלֶךְ, אִי אֶפְשָׁר לוֹ לְבֵן לְנַתֵּק הַקֶּשֶׁר עִם אָבִיו.

אם אַחֵינוּ נִמְצָאִים בְּסַכָּנָה אֵין אָנוּ בָּאִים חָלִילָה בְּתַרְעוֹמֶת וּבִטְעָנָה לְפָנֶיךָ, כִּי כָל מִשְׁפָּטֶיךָ אֱמֶת צָדְקוּ יַחְדָּו, וּכְמַאֲמַר הַכָּתוּב (דברים לב, ד) 'הַצּוּר תָּמִים פָּעֳלוֹ, כִּי כָל דְּרָכָיו מִשְׁפָּט, אֵל אֱמוּנָה וְאֵין עָוֶל, צַדִּיק וְיָשָׁר הוּא'. אָמְנָם בְּכָל זֹאת מֻכְרָחִים אָנוּ לְהַבִּיעַ גֹּדֶל צַעֲרֵנוּ, וּלְהִתְחַנֵּן לְפָנֶיךָ לַהֲפֹךְ אֶת הַדִּין. אָנָּא הֱיֵה 'אָבִינוּ' תְּחִילָה וְאַחַר כָּךְ 'מַלְכֵּנוּ'. גַּלֵּה אַהֲבָתְךָ וְרַחֲמֶיךָ הָרַבִּים תְּחִילָה, וּמִשְׁפָּטֶיךָ רַק לְאַחַר מִכֵּן. הֲלֹא אִם אָנוּ מִתְחַנְּנִים לְפָנֶיךָ כְּבָנִים, כְּאָח בְּעַד אָחִיו, לָמָּה לֹא תַּעֲנֵינוּ אַתָּה - בְּמִדָּה כְּנֶגֶד מִדָּה - בְּמִדַּת הָרַחֲמִים, כְּאָב רַחֲמָן, וְלֹא בְּמִדַּת הַדִּין כְּמֶלֶךְ?

אָנָּא תֵּן לָנוּ לְהִתְעוֹרֵר מִלְמַטָּה. תֵּן לִכְנֶסֶת יִשְׂרָאֵל - בְּנֵי מִשְׁפַּחְתֵּנוּ - לְהִתְקָרֵב אֵלֶיךָ וּלְהִתְדַּבֵּק בָּךְ עַל יְדֵי מַעֲשֵׂיהֶם הַטּוֹבִים, וְלֹא עַל יְדֵי יִסּוּרִים וּמִיתַת צַדִּיקִים, חָלִילָה. תֵּן לָנוּ הַגְּבוּרָה וְהָעוֹז שֶׁנּוּכַל לִזְכּוֹת לְהַשְׁרָאַת שְׁכִינָתְךָ אַחַת וּלְתָמִיד, עַל יְדֵי מַעֲשֵׂינוּ אָנוּ. תֵּן לָנוּ שֶׁנּוּכַל לָלֶכֶת לִקְרַאת הַגְּאוּלָה בְּקוֹמָה זְקוּפָה, כָּרָאוּי לִבְנֵי מְלָכִים.

זַכֵּנוּ בְּצַדִּיקֵי אֱמֶת וּבְמַנְהִיגִים הָרְאוּיִים לְאוֹתָהּ אִיצְטְלָא שֶׁיַּדְרִיכוּ אוֹתָנוּ וְיוֹרוּ לָנוּ אֶת הַדֶּרֶךְ אֲשֶׁר נֵלֵךְ בָּהּ עַד שׁוּבֵנוּ אֵלֶיךָ בֶּאֱמֶת. תֵּן לָנוּ שֶׁנִּהְיֶה רְאוּיִים לְקַבֵּל אוֹרְךָ וְטוּבְךָ שֶׁרָצִיתָ לְהֵיטִיב לָנוּ וְשִׂמְחַת עוֹלָם עַל רֹאשֵׁינוּ, וְיִהְיֶה שָׁלוֹם בֶּאֱמֶת בְּעָלְמָא הָדֵין וּבְעָלְמָא דְּאָתֵי. אָמֵן כֵּן יְהִי רָצוֹן.

לִישׁוּעָתְךָ קִוִּיתִי ה':

ABRIDGED ACHDUS PRAYER

Master of the Universe, My Father, My King!

I declare before You that I have been truly blind. I have slandered my fellow Jew and through this evil deed, I have become an enemy to myself and to him since I have empowered heavenly accusations against both of us. I pray that my slander should be disregarded since it is only an indication of my smallness and I sincerely disallow my slander to cast an evil eye upon him.

I have also been blind to one of Your greatest truths. That every Jew, whoever and wherever they are, is in reality my brother and sister and that we are as one family before You, our Eternal Father.

Instead, I have treated my fellow Jew as a stranger and even sometimes, as an enemy. In my arrogance I felt superior to him If I disagreed with him, then I should have prayed for him and not denigrated him.

Woe is me that I have been blind to the pain of my brother and to the pain of my Father.

However, I declare before You today that I am no longer blind. I feel that all my fellow Jews are my brothers and sisters.

Furthermore, I have now become truly aware of my brother's sufferings and dangers. I sincerely cry out for my brother's and sister's sake, and I beg You to be merciful to them as our Father. Save my brothers and sisters worldwide from the twin plagues of assimilation and intermarriage. I cannot bear to see the lost. Are they not my family, Your children??

Give them a new light so they can return to You, their Eternal Father.

Save my brothers and sisters in the land of Israel. Even here, where I am out of harm's way, I have no peace of mind while they are in danger. Save them from the evil designs of the *Eirev Rav, Yishmael* and *Esav.*

Restrain Your anger from those who are closest to You, those who observe Your Torah. How many of their young must die? How many orphans must they count?

Save them for they have suffered tremendously. Open their eyes to the pain of a Father so that they can use the power of their prayers to redeem their fellow Jews.

I do not criticize You for my brother's dangers since Your ways are all just and perfect.

Still, I must cry out to You from my pain. Be our Father first, showing mercy and our King second. If we cry to You as children, a brother for a brother, shall You not, measure for measure, respond to us first as a Father and not as a King?

Let my family have an awakening from below with leadership that can guide them to this.

Let us earn Your Presence with heads held high. Finally, grant us Your light so that we can have true peace in this world and in the next.

Amen, may this be Your will.

תְּפִלַּת הָאָח

הַמַּהֲדוּרָה הַקְּצָרָה

רִבּוֹן הָעוֹלָמִים

אָבִינוּ מַלְכֵּנוּ, בָּאתִי לְהִתְחַנֵּן וּלְהִתְוַדּוֹת לְפָנֶיךָ עַל שֶׁזֶּה הַרְבֵּה שָׁנִים טָחוּ עֵינַי מֵרְאוֹת אֶת הָאֱמֶת וּכְעִוֵּר הַמְגַשֵּׁשׁ בָּאֲפֵלָה הָיִיתִי. הָלַכְתִּי רָכִיל וְדִבַּרְתִּי לָשׁוֹן הָרַע עַל בְּנֵי עַמִּי, וּבָזֶה נָתַתִּי כֹּחַ וְעוֹז לַשָּׂטָן, הַמְקַטְרֵג הַגָּדוֹל, לְהָבִיא צְרוֹר חֲטָאַי וּפְשָׁעַי לִפְנֵי כִּסֵּא הַדִּין שֶׁבְּבֵית דִּינְךָ הַצֶּדֶק וְלֹא זָכִיתִי לְחַנְּנָתְךָ בְּרַחֲמֶיךָ הָרַבִּים וּלְשְׁמִירָתְךָ הָעֶלְיוֹנָה מִמִּדַּת הַדִּין הַתַּקִּיפָה. **עוֹד** רָעָה גְדוֹלָה מִזוֹ הִיא מַה שֶּׁגָּרְמָה הַלָּשׁוֹן הָרַע שֶׁלִּי לַחֲבֵרַי, שֶׁשַּׂמְתִּי עָלָיו עַיִן רָעָה, וּבָזֶה הִכְרַחְתִּי גַּם אוֹתוֹ לַעֲמוֹד לִפְנֵי כִּסֵּא הַדִּין. הַלְוַאי וְיָדַעְתִּי כֹּחַ הָאֶרֶס שֶׁבְּפִי וּלְשׁוֹנִי וְשֶׁהַמָּוֶת וְהַחַיִּים בְּיַד הַלָּשׁוֹן (עי' משלי יח, כא). אִם דִּבַּרְתִּי עָלָיו לָשׁוֹן הָרַע וּרְכִילוּת הֲרֵי זֶה רַק מֵחֲמַת קַטְנוּתִי וְקִנְאַת אִישׁ מֵרֵעֵהוּ, אֲבָל חַס וְחָלִילָה שֶׁיִּיגָּרֵם לַחֲבֵרַי שׁוּם נֶזֶק עַל יָדִי כְּלָל. וַאֲנִי מִתְחָרֵט עַל זֶה חֲרָטָה גְמוּרָה וּמְקַבֵּל אֲנִי עַל עַצְמִי מֵהַיּוֹם וָהָלְאָה לִשְׁמוֹר פִּי וּלְשׁוֹנִי וְלֹא לָשׁוּב לְכִסְלָה עוֹד.

הַדָּבָר הַגָּרוּעַ בְּיוֹתֵר שֶׁעוֹלֵל לִי הָעִוָּרוֹן הוּא שֶׁזֶּה מָנַע מִמֶּנִּי הַהַכָּרָה בְּאַחַת מִן הָאֲמִתִּיּוֹת הַגְּדוֹלוֹת שֶׁבָּעוֹלָם: **שֶׁכָּל יְהוּדִי וִיהוּדִי, יִהְיֶה מִי שֶׁיִּהְיֶה וּבְאֵיזֶה מַצָּב שֶׁיִּהְיֶה, הוּא בֶּאֱמֶת אָחִי וְאֲחוֹתִי, בָּשָׂר מִבְּשָׂרִי, וְשְׁכֻלָּנוּ בְּנֵי מִשְׁפָּחָה אַחַת בְּעֵינֶיךָ, אָבִינוּ שֶׁבַּשָּׁמַיִם. בְּגַאֲוָתִי**, הִרְגַּשְׁתִּי עֶלְיוֹנוּת עָלָיו וְלָכֵן הִתְיַחַסְתִּי אֵלָיו בְּגַאֲוָה וָבוּז, וְלֹא רָאִיתִי בְּצַעֲרוֹ וְלֹא הִשְׁגַּחְתִּי עַל גּוֹדֶל

הַכְּאֵב שֶׁלְּךָ. אוֹי לוֹ לְאָח שֶׁעֵינָיו סְתוּמוֹת מִלְּהַרְגִּישׁ בְּצַעַר אָחִיו, וְאוֹי לוֹ לְבֵן שֶׁעֵינָיו סְתוּמוֹת מִלִּרְאוֹת בְּצַעַר אָבִיו.

אָמְנָם בָּאתִי לוֹמַר לְפָנֶיךָ שֶׁכְּבָר נִפְקְחוּ עֵינַי, וְהָעִוָּרוֹן שֶׁלִּי חָלַף הָלַךְ לוֹ. אָמְנָם מֻכְרָח אֲנִי לוֹמַר שֶׁהַהַשְׁקָפָה זוֹ גּוֹרֶמֶת לִי הַרְבֵּה צַעַר וְעָגְמַת נֶפֶשׁ. כִּי לָרִאשׁוֹנָה יוֹאנִי רוֹאֶה בֶּאֱמֶת אֶת צַעֲרוֹ וּכְאֵבוֹ שֶׁל אָחִי, וַאֲנִי מַרְגִּישׁ בְּסַכָּנוֹת הָאֲיוּמוֹת שֶׁהוּא שָׁרוּי בָּהּ. וְעַתָּה אָבִינוּ, אָב רַחוּם וְחַנּוּן, הִנְנִי שׁוֹפֵךְ לְפָנֶיךָ לֵב כַּמַּיִם וְצוֹעֵק לְמַעַן אָחִי כְּאָח הַמַּרְגִּישׁ וּמִצְטַעֵר בְּצַעַר אָחִיו, וַאֲנִי מְבַקֵּשׁ מִמְּךָ שֶׁתִּשְׁמַע וּתְקַבֵּל צַעֲקָתִי, שֶׁהֲרֵי אַתָּה הָאָב שֶׁל שְׁנֵינוּ. הַצֵּל נָא אֶת אָחִי וּפְדֵה אוֹתוֹ מִכָּל צָרוֹתָיו בְּעוֹד מוֹעֵד, כִּי הוּא בְּצָרָה גְּדוֹלָה מְאֹד.

למען אחב"י שנתערבו בגויים:

לִבִּי מֵיצַר וְדוֹאֵב, בִּרְאוֹתִי בְּאָבְדַן מִלְיוֹנֵי אַחֵינוּ בְּנֵי יִשְׂרָאֵל בְּכָל קְצָוֵי תֵּבֵל לְמַכַּת הַהִתְבּוֹלְלוּת וְנִשּׂוּאֵי תַּעֲרוֹבֶת, רַחֲמָנָא לִיצְּלָן. אֵיךְ נוּכַל לִרְאוֹת בְּאָבְדַן כָּל כָּךְ הַרְבֵּה אַחִים וַאֲחָיוֹת, נְשָׁמוֹת אוֹבְדוֹת לַאֲבִיהֶם שֶׁבַּשָּׁמַיִם. וְכִי לָאו בְּנֵי מִשְׁפַּחְתִּי הֵם? הַאִם אֵינְךָ אֲבִיהֶם? אָנָּא תָּעֳרֶה עֲלֵיהֶם רוּחַ מִמָּרוֹם כְּדֵי שֶׁיּוּכְלוּ לְהַכִּיר בְּבֵרוּר אֶת אֲבִיהֶם שֶׁבַּשָּׁמַיִם.

למען אחב"י בארה"ק:

הַצֵּל נָא אֶת אַחֵינוּ בְּנֵי יִשְׂרָאֵל תּוֹשְׁבֵי אַרְצֵנוּ הַקְּדוֹשָׁה הַחַיִּים בִּדְאָגָה וּבֶחֳרָדָה מִדֵּי יוֹם בְּיוֹמוֹ מִפַּחַד הָאוֹיְבִים, זֶרַע יִשְׁמָעֵאל, אֲשֶׁר אוֹרְבִים לְחַיֵּיהֶם תָּמִיד. אֵיךְ נִמְצָא מַרְגּוֹעַ לְנַפְשֵׁנוּ כַּאן בִּמְקוֹמוֹת מוֹשְׁבוֹתֵנוּ אַף שֶׁאָנוּ חַיִּים בֶּטַח וְשַׁאֲנָן, בְּשָׁעָה שֶׁאַחֵינוּ שֶׁבְּאֶרֶץ יִשְׂרָאֵל מֻקָּפִים מֵאוֹיְבִים צְמֵאֵי דָם. אָנָּא הַצֵּל אוֹתָם בְּעוֹד מוֹעֵד מֵהַיָּדַיִם הָאַכְזָרִיִּים שֶׁל זֶרַע יִשְׁמָעֵאל, עֵשָׂו וְהָעֵרֶב רַב.

למען אחב"י שומרי תורה ומצוות:

הָשֵׁב כַּעַסְךָ וַחֲרוֹן אַפְּךָ מִבָּנֶיךָ שׁוֹמְרֵי תּוֹרָתְךָ וּמִצְוֹתֶיךָ, הַקְּרוֹבִים אֵלֶיךָ בְּיוֹתֵר. אָנָּא, אַל יָמוּתוּ צְעִירֵיהֶם בִּדְמִי יְמֵיהֶם. כַּמָּה יְתוֹמִים צְרִיכִים הֵם לְמָנוֹת? כַּמָּה חוֹלִי צְרִיכִים הֵם לִסְבּוֹל? הַאִם לֹא נִתְמַלֵּא כְּבָר כּוֹס צָרָתָם? אָנָּא פְּתַח עֵינֵיהֶם וְתֵן לָהֶם לִרְאוֹת בְּצַעֲרוֹ שֶׁל הָאָב. תֵּן לָהֶם שֶׁיִּנָּצְלוּ אֶת כֹּחַ הַתְּפִלָּה שֶׁלָּהֶם לִפְדוֹת שְׁאָר בָּנֶיךָ שֶׁאֵינָם יוֹדְעִים מְאוּמָה וּלְהָאִיר מְאוֹרְךָ עֲלֵיהֶם. אָנָּא רַחֵם עֲלֵיהֶם וְאַל תְּהִי מִדַּת הַדִּין מְתוּחָה עֲלֵיהֶם עוֹד, כִּי הֵם רַק בָּשָׂר וָדָם. הֲלֹא הֵמָּה בָּנֶיךָ וִידִידֶיךָ הַנֶּאֱמָנִים לְךָ בְּיוֹתֵר.

אִם אַחֵינוּ בְּנֵי יִשְׂרָאֵל נִמְצָאִים בְּסַכָּנָה אֵין אֲנִי בָּא חָלִילָה בְּתַרְעוֹמֶת וּבִטְעָנָה לְפָנֶיךָ, וּכְמַאֲמַר הַכָּתוּב (דברים לב, ד) 'הַצּוּר תָּמִים פָּעֳלוֹ, כִּי כָל דְּרָכָיו מִשְׁפָּט, אֵל אֱמוּנָה וְאֵין עָוֶל, צַדִּיק וְיָשָׁר הוּא'. אָמְנָם בְּכָל זֹאת מוּכְרָח אֲנִי לְהַבִּיעַ גּוֹדֶל צַעֲרִי וּלְהִתְחַנֵּן לְפָנֶיךָ לַהֲפוֹךְ אֶת הַדִּין. אָנָּא הֱיֵה 'אָבִינוּ' תְּחִילָּה וְאַחַר כַּךְ 'מַלְכֵּנוּ'. אִם אֲנִי מִתְחַנֵּן לְפָנֶיךָ כְּבֵן, כְּאָח בְּעַד אָחִיו, לָמָּה לֹא תַּעֲנֵנוּ אַתָּה בְּמִדָּה כְּנֶגֶד מִדָּה - בְּמִדַּת הָרַחֲמִים, כְּאָב רַחֲמָן, וְלֹא בְּמִדַּת הַדִּין כְּמֶלֶךְ?!

אָנָּא תֵּן לָנוּ לְהִתְעוֹרֵר מִלְּמַטָּה. תֵּן לִכְנֶסֶת יִשְׂרָאֵל - בְּנֵי מִשְׁפַּחְתִּי - לְהִתְקָרֵב אֵלֶיךָ וּלְהִתְדַּבֵּק בְּךָ עַל יְדֵי מַעֲשֵׂיהֶם הַטּוֹבִים, וְלֹא עַל יְדֵי יִסּוּרִים וּמִיתַת צַדִּיקִים, חָלִילָה. תֵּן לָנוּ שֶׁנִּהְיֶה רְאוּיִים לְקַבֵּל אוֹרְךָ וְטוּבְךָ שֶׁרָצִיתָ לְהֵיטִיב לָנוּ וְשִׂמְחַת עוֹלָם עַל רֹאשֵׁנוּ, וְיִהְיֶה שָׁלוֹם בֶּאֱמֶת בְּעָלְמָא הָדֵין וּבְעָלְמָא דְּאָתֵי. אָמֵן כֵּן יְהִי רָצוֹן.

לִישׁוּעָתְךָ קִוִּיתִי ה':

Dear Reader,

Thank you for joining us on this enlightening journey. We hope that you have found it thought-provoking, inspiring, and a motive to be more mindful and careful with the mitzvah of shmirat halashon.

If you have any questions, comments, or insights you'd like to share, we would be delighted to hear from you. Please don't hesitate to reach out to us at nissim@powerjews.com; your engagement and feedback are invaluable to us.

We also encourage you to share this book with others who may benefit from its teachings. By spreading the word and engaging in meaningful discussions about the mitzvah of *shmirat halashon* (guarding one's speech), we can collectively bring the Redemption.

Furthermore, if you feel compelled to contribute to the further distribution of this book and help us in our mission to spread these important ideas to *Klal Yisroel*, we welcome your support. Every donation, no matter the size, makes a significant impact in reaching a wider audience and fostering true *achdus* (unity) among us all.

Together, let us continue striving towards a world where these concepts are embraced by all, paving the way for the coming of the Mashiach and the ultimate fulfillment of our shared destiny.

If you have enjoyed the work of Rabbi Shimon Kessin Shlit"a, and would like to learn more from the Rabbi, many of his shiurim available online.

Scan the link below to access the different platforms Rabbi Kessin is on:

www.torahanytime.com/#/speaker?l=93
www.youtube.com/@hashkafadotorg707
www.hashkafa.org

With deep gratitude and heartfelt blessings

Get Inspired and Inspire Others!

If you felt inspired by these pages, it's because a previous donor generously supported our cause. We encourage you to continue this chain of inspiration by empowering another with free Torah content. You never know whom you might inspire, and in turn, who they might inspire—all because of you.

PowerJews.com

Made in the USA
Monee, IL
17 November 2024